"Verge has a unique ability to turn complex financial concepts into simple visual ideas that "jump to life". He shows us how to understand and profit from complex global deflation concepts in a very unique and engaging style. This is the first financial book that I would consider a 'page turner'. So put on Verge's deflation sunglasses and enjoy the view. I am confident that you will profit from the experience. I recommend it."

-Tom Courteau, CIM

Vice President, Investment Advisor, Portfolio Manager
The Courteau Wealth Management Team
Richardson GMP Limited

Table of Contents

Chapter 3 - Visions of the Future

Lift off for GOLD ?
The Chinese Have …. ***the Pin!***

Chapter 4 - How to Profit Now!

To **truly** Profit from Deflation, you must understand
HUBRIS
Cash Is King !
Deflationary '20/20 Vision'
What Comes First - Unemployment or Deflation ?
What if 'Net Present Value' goes in Reverse?
The Future of Retail is 'Showrooms and Phones'
Real Estate: 'Gateway Cities and Micro Pockets'
Hometown Refugees
Why Gold is Bi-Polar
The 'Expected Value' of Gold
How Much Would You Pay For An Extra Year of Life?
"The value of time inflates over time!"
How to Profit Now With Your...***wait for it***...'Personal
Prescription *In-Deflation* Sunglasses'
Service Inflation and Commodity Deflation, A once in a
lifetime opportunity
'Inflation Island'
Scenario Planning
    Base Case: Phase One: **Global Deflation**
        Phase Two: ***The great American Decade Ahead***
    Worst Case
Action Plans!

Chapter 5 – Summary

About the Author

Endnotes

Acknowledgments

During the writing of this book I could find no one who agreed with me. Everyone I spoke to said that I was way out in left field. Not one person agreed with me or would help me. They all asked me where I did my research, where did I get such nonsensical ideas. No one supported me.

It is to those people that I firstly express my thanks. Without them this book would not have been created. If everyone had agreed with me, I would not have felt like I had uncovered an original idea. But because so many people disagreed with me so vehemently, I knew I had a unique idea, something worth pursuing, so on I went. I put on my 'Tin foil hat' and kept writing.

On a positive note, I would like to thank all my business associates and friends who worked with me on this project. And thanks to my early readers for the gifts of their time and intelligence. Their comments on early drafts of the document kept me on track. But most of all, I would like to thank my immediate family, Barb, Brent, and Danielle. Without your support and creative feedback, I would not have had the drive to finish the job. Thank you all.

Introduction

Global Deflation: and *The Next Great American Decade!*

Deflation cannot be fully understood if considered only from a local perspective. Since the actions from one country can drastically affect another, deflation can only be understood from a global perspective. When looked at globally, the world is in the middle of the greatest deflationary period in a generation. This can be seen in the deflationary spiral of commodities and the massive devaluation of global currencies. (I believe that currency devaluation **is** deflation.) However each country in the world is in a different phase of their own deflationary 'Mini-cycle'. If you assume that a deflationary cycle can take ten years to complete, some countries are just about to enter their deflationary decade while others, like the United States, are just now reaching their escape velocities. It is the deflationary interrelationships between countries in different parts of the cycle that has created one of the biggest opportunities for America in a generation.

Most observers will not see the opportunities unfolding in front of them because deflation is such an unknown science that they can't 'read the tea leaves' of change. Since the great depression of 1929, international governments have misdirected the population to focus only on inflation and growth. But deflation and consolidation are equal partners in the business cycle and need to be given equal understanding. This book will show you new ways to look at the situation. It will show you how inflation and deflation are on the same continuum, how each country has different needs based upon where they are in their own deflation cycle, and how countries manipulate each other by exporting deflation. It will show you how the U.S. Central Bank has been unwillingly coerced into becoming 'Central Bank to the World', and it will show you how this confluence of situations has come together to create the opportunity of a generation for America. Finally it will show you how to profit from this 'perfect economic storm'.

Right now the world is the middle of the greatest war of all time, a deflationary war. Some countries are fighting for survival and others for dominance. The weapons of choice are not bombs or bullets or drones, they are interest rates, commodity prices and capital investments. This book goes beyond interest rates and currency wars, it delves into the dark science of game theory, international intimidation, and Mutual Assured Destruction (MAD). The Cold War is back on, but this time the 'Weapons of Mass Destruction' are financial.

Over the past decades most economists have shunned the study of deflation because they would much prefer to study and support government inflationary policies. However, over the next decade, many countries of the world will fall into deep periods of deflation and will need new tools to deal with it. Most observers do not have the understanding required to 'read the global deflationary tea leaves'. In this book I will attempt to arm the reader with new models and tools to better look at the inflation and deflation detailed data in order to see the bigger picture. I refer to these models as 'deflation sunglasses'. Go ahead and put them on. I hope you enjoy the view.

Only The Essentials - No Fluff

I am not an economist. I think that is a good thing. I am however, very good with numbers and pattern recognition. I like the eloquence of a good mathematical formula as much as the next guy, but I don't find that they add much value to our daily lives. I prefer to think in terms of simple visual models and images. Things that don't make too much sense to me as formulas seem to 'pop' when converted to images. Going "0 to

220 miles per hour in eight seconds" takes on much more meaning for me when I see the image of a dragster blasting down a dragstrip. I find that visual models and images are more intuitive and help me understand life instantaneously.

Economics, however, is a hobby of mine. I engage in it every day and I try to make sense of the world. However, I find it hard to understand all the nuances, mathematical complexities and numbers that the supposed experts throw around. I also find that people use one set of logic to prove one position, and then use the same logic later to support a different position. It also concerns me that the experts don't even seem to agree on the parameters to use when evaluating a set of data. Some people on a committee vote for one direction and others vote the other way. Shouldn't there be only one right way? In general I am not sure all the pundits know the implications of what they are suggesting. I am also not sure the average person even understands what these pundits are saying.

Because the pundits aren't sure of what they are doing, they make up for it in volume and frequency. The retail and internet stores are full of millions of financial books and publications. These documents are quite diverse and often espouse conflicting positions. This book is intended to boil down all the noise out there into **only the essential things you need to understand**. I am sure you have heard the old saying often attributed to Blaise Pascal, the French philosopher, "I am sorry to have wearied you with so long a letter, but I didn't have time to write you a short one" (Ramer, 2011, p. 315-316). This book is intended to be the 'short one'. There is no 'fluff' in this book.

To boil down all this information into a small understandable package, I have had to create a few new economic models. I think part of the current complexity problem is that existing models and formulas that were made to investigate old sets of problems are being used to address new sets of problems. Although they are technically still accurate, they add no insight

11

to the problem at hand, and they come with lots of frivolous explanation (a.k.a. fluff). Basically they don't fit. I am a firm believer that if you build the right model for a problem, it can simplify the problem so much that the solutions become obvious. You may not agree with all the models or assumptions in this book, but please consider them with an open mind. They will definitely give you a new way of looking at things. I think you will find that with the new paradigms, everything will become more clear and intuitive. This is a short book on purpose.

The power of problem modeling is often best shown with an example. Consider this one.

Suppose you had five hundred people in a large gymnasium and you were asked to create a basketball team. You had all the data on each individual. How would you organize the problem? You could group everybody by hair color. But that probably would not help you much. You could group everybody by weight. That might help you a little, but not enough. Or you could group everybody by height. That might help you a lot. If you lined up everybody by height, you immediately and obviously see some possible solutions. But if you were asked to put together a female team, separating the gender would have been very productive at the beginning, before you organized by height. Leaving both genders in the model actually increased the complexity more than was necessary. So the point is that models can be very insightful if they are designed to solve the correct problem at hand. They can also be counterproductive if they were designed to solve the wrong problem. The trick is to find the smallest model that most accurately reflects the specific problem you are trying to solve. If you succeed in this, it can be very enlightening.

I believe that economists are making their current tasks more difficult by working with outdated models that are counterproductive. My goal in this book is to expose you to a few new intuitive models that can simplify some of the economic problems that we are all facing today. That way you will be able to make educated decisions on your own. You will know who to believe, what is actually happening and then profit from the results. With these new models you should be able to more clearly 'see' the problems and also see the implications of future actions. At the end of this small but concentrated book, I would hope that you will develop your own simple visualizations to handle next year's problems.

I believe that the biggest economic problem we face in the world today is leverage, also known as debt. As individuals and governments, we are now at our collective credit limits, and in many cases well past. With all the monetary and fiscal stimulus initiatives over the past thirty years, we have reached the max. What do we do now? Do we print more money? Do we go with austerity? Both? Whatever we decide to do collectively will show up in one major indicator, the inflation metric. All the decisions we make individually and collectively will show up in this inflation statistic, whether it shows up as inflation or deflation.

People talk about inflation or deflation as separate items. The first key new concept of this book is that inflation and deflation are on the same continuum. They should be considered in the same thought. They are the same thing. Just like temperature relates to freezing and thawing, deflation is just negative inflation. In the concept of the inflation-deflation bell curve you will see later in this book that, although, at the time of printing, overall inflation rate is positive, many items are deflating. And as we move along the bell curve toward the left, more and more items deflate. Moving to the right, more items inflate. Knowing what will inflate and what will deflate is the key to profiting in the future.
There is no single word for the concept that inflation and deflation are on the same curve. So I will use the word 'In-deflation'. Knowing where individual items are on the curve,

and knowing where you, personally, are on the curve can make all the difference to your future success.

The second key concept of this book is that in-deflation can only be understood if you look at it from a global perspective. Inflation is relative. Countries inflate or deflate their economies in relation to each other. One country may devalue their currency thereby causing inflation locally (importing inflation) and causing deflation to others (exporting deflation). One of the biggest mistake economists are making today is to look at inflation from only the local currency perspective. The constant measurement metric for all in-deflation discussions should be the U.S. Dollar. It has been recognized all over the world for the past one hundred years as the world's reserve currency. I believe all other currencies are currently still 'experimental'.

Of course this is all more complicated since all of this is happening in the ever-accelerating world of global finance and communications. It is getting more and more difficult to separate the signal from the noise. Twenty-five years ago when I completed my MBA, we were trained to craft five-year strategic plans using traditional mathematical tools like algebra and statistics. Although that is still a base line requirement, it is not enough to ensure success in today's fast paced world. Today one must consider chaos theory, scenario planning, and game theory as well. Instead of firing off a strategic planning rocket and letting it fly unaided, like we did twenty years ago, today's strategic planning is more like a poker game where you have already considered all your competitor's possible moves, and you are ready to change direction on a moment's notice. You need to know how gas fracking in South Dakota will affect the presidential elections in Russia. You need to know how the building of micro homes in Japan can predict house prices in Detroit. And you need to know it in real time. To do all this, yes you need your five-year strategic plan, but you also need some of the instantaneous visual models described in this book.

As we continue, it will be helpful to understand how this book is organized. Chapter One deals with inflation and deflation as we know it today. Chapter Two offers some new models to help us deal with tomorrow's problems. Models like the inflation-deflation continuum help us deal with tomorrow's inflation problems. To make money from inflation or deflation in the future, I believe that you must consider them both at once. Considering them separately is to miss the opportunity. Chapter Three extrapolates on the models discussed in order to create a few inflationary "visions of the future". It also offers some guidelines on strategic planning for the future. Chapter Four offers more specific suggestions on how to profit from the next great deflationary period. There is a lot to cover. But first, let me try to explain why the study of deflation is not in vogue today.

Tin Foil Hats

If you search the internet, you will find about ten times as many references to inflation as opposed to deflation. You are probably thinking that if deflation is so debilitating and so probable, why is no one talking about it? Why should I worry about it?

That is the question that I had in researching this book. Why are there no government pundits willing to talk about it or suggesting how to prepare for it? Why are there so few web sites on the topic? Why are there no financial charts showing the 'Present Value' of money for when interest rates are negative? Do people think we won't go there? Do people think it won't happen? Since 1981 interest rates have come down sixteen percent from seventeen percent to one percent. Do people think it is not possible to go to zero or negative one in the next year or two? Every talking head in the media refers to "when things get back to normal...", or "We are seeing a slow start to next year followed by six months of growth". Why is it not possible for us to have six months of slow growth followed by six months of negative growth? Well, one of the reasons is that all the pundits have a vested interest in inflation. They are either sponsored by one or more governments that are depending on inflation for survival, or they are selling financial products or stocks that depend on inflation. What would happen to stock prices if the pundits started telling the truth, that there is a chance that we may enter a five to ten year period of one to four percent deflation. What would happen to their job security.

The only people who are sounding any warning bells are the people who sell gold products or gold funds. And that is another suspect investment class that is a topic for later in the book.

The 'Tin Foil Hat' was a concept mentioned in a science fiction story by Julian Huxley, (1927) "The Tissue-Culture King". It was a concept where a piece of headgear was made from one or more sheets of aluminum foil and worn on the head to protect the brain from electromagnetic fields, mind control, or mind reading. Later it evolved into 'The Tin Foil Hat Society'. This was a group of individuals who agreed to wear tin foil hats to be sure to be free from government or alien influence. In talking to individuals and groups around the country I sometimes feel that I am the only one studying the deflation possibility. I feel like I am the only member of the 'Tin Foil Hat Society on Deflation'. Everyone else seems to be accepting the government bureaucratic position of continuing inflation like it is a non-event. No one seems to realize that should deflation occur and we are not prepared, it could be the single most debilitating financial occurrence in our lifetimes. However, if we are prepared, it could be financially very rewarding. I get the feeling like the government and financial institutions feel that declaring deflation a possibility would be like yelling "fire" in a crowded movie theatre. Everyone would head for the exits in mass panic, with many getting trampled along the way. This book is intended to introduce deflation in a measured way so that we can all escape financially well prepared.

Inflation Colored Sunglasses – Opportunity of a Lifetime?

I mentioned that I prefer visions, images and models to help me understand complex issues. So try this one on for size. Imagine you are walking down the road and you stumble across a pair of big sunglasses on the ground. They are wild and glitzy sunglasses. You put them on and you find that they are magic sunglasses. They are inflation sunglasses. They let you look at an item and you can see how much the price will change one year from now. You walk into a supermarket and look at the oranges. The sunglasses say -5%. You look at the bananas and the glasses say +3%. You look at the bread and the glasses say -8%. You walk down the street and the glasses say: German car +2%. Japanese car -6%. House in the suburbs -3%. Imagine if you had the ability to look at things and predict the cost a year from now. You would buy the gainers and rent the losers. That is how you prosper in the future.

I hope to create some new models for you that will help you to instantly make sense of the upcoming inflation – deflation world. You will see that certain products are inflating at the same time that others are deflating. You will also see that some countries are inflating while others are deflating. In fact, in order to make sense of what's happening you must look economics from a global perspective. You will see how countries can import inflation and export deflation at the same time. By looking at deflation from a global perspective I hope you will be able to see the upcoming "in-deflation opportunity of a lifetime" just over the horizon. Regardless of what happens it is my hope that the ideas and models discussed in this book will help you to make sense of our complex inflation-deflation world.

People have been taught to fear the great deflationary death spiral. There is no need for that if you understand it and use it to your advantage. It can be a boon to you. For example, "Would you buy this book today if it were 7% cheaper next year?" Just kidding. Of course you would, because it can make you money right now because knowledge is power.

So sit back. Put the sunglasses on, and enjoy the view. You will be making profitable decisions in the blink of an eye.

Chapter 1. Old Inflation Models

I Am Not Prepared For This.

From time to time I have this recurring dream…….

That's when it hit me. I went to the bank to make a deposit and they wanted to charge me a 'storage fee' on my cash. They wanted to charge me negative interest rates. They said that because prices were falling globally, they couldn't pay me any interest. I was lucky to be able to store my money there and that the storage fee was so small.

What was I to do? Should I store all my cash at my house? Would it be safe? If everybody did that would there be a higher incidence of house break-ins? Would crime go up? Are the authorities prepared for the pending crime waves? Would there be a run on the banks? Would the government announce a 'bank holiday' and shut the banks? I had watched this economic crisis develop over the past few years as if in slow motion. But that's when it finally hit me. 'I'm not prepared for this.'

………..I begin to wonder what it would be like if interest rates were negative.

Imagine for a moment, going down to the shore of a major river every day after dinner to watch the boats go by. For thirty years you watched as the river slowly rolled by from left to right at steady and predictable pace. Over the years that pace varied depending on weather conditions, the winter snowfall, ice conditions, and other factors. Then imagine one day you went down for your after dinner stroll and you noticed the strangest thing. You noticed that the river was slowing down a little. It had slowed down from five miles per hour to three miles per hour. Although that was quite remarkable, it had happened before and was not cause for alarm. It just meant that the water would move a little slower, the swimming would be a little easier and the barges would take a little longer to reach their destinations. This river had been rolling along for many many years. Stranger things had happened.

You go back a few days later and the river had slowed down to one mile per hour. This would be a bit of a concern because the river would be a little harder to navigate, the water might turn a little more brackish, and the barges would take longer to arrive. But the government would decide that the river was too important to the economy and would begin pumping in more water and dredge the middle of the channels to ensure continuing commerce.

But then imagine, the next day you go back to the river's edge, and you see that the water is flowing in the opposite direction! The water is flowing from right to left. Immediately it hits you, "now this is a problem". This is a problem on many levels. Not only do you know that the water is going the wrong way. You know that the plumbing is all wrong. The plumbing has been set up for left to right. Now it means that all the water will be flowing upstream causing back ups and floods. Water would be streaming out of sewers, out of toilets, over river banks. All the plumbing that had been built up over hundreds of years was designed for water flowing in the opposite direction. The pipes, the pumps, the valves, were all designed for 'left to right flow'. They are no help to you now. They were designed for another era. And what about all the barges that would float down the river with the current. When the river slowed from five miles per hour to one mile per hour, (a four mile per hour change), it meant that the barges would

20

be a little late or carry a little less. When the river went from plus one mile per hour to minus one mile per hour,(only a two mile per hour change) it meant that the barges would never arrive! In fact it meant that they would be going in the other direction, and may be lost forever. Barges, boats and commerce in general, that were initiated optimistically under the old conditions, were now in peril under the new conditions.

You may already have guessed that the river in this example is meant to be the economy and the flow rate is meant to represent the inflation rate. For the past thirty years we have gone to the edge of the river and watched the inflation rate slow from twelve percent to eight percent to four percent and recently down to one percent. All the while we have watched as the government has pumped in more water (money) but still the inflation rate slows. People talk about "when the inflation rate gets back to normal". But what is normal? Is eight percent normal? Is one percent normal? Or is minus one percent normal? No one knows the answer to that question. We just know what we have experienced. For most of us, that has been inflation.

It is important to remember that there is a whole other world of possibilities in our economic future. A world where prices go down, wages go down, assets go down, and currency values go up, and inflation .... goes negative. It's called deflation. Many people fear it, governments loath it. Very few remember it. But one thing is certain, when inflation goes below zero, many of the financial, administrative plumbing systems that we built up during the last fifty years of inflation will fail. They were all designed for inflationary times. Deflation was not even in the thought process. Inflation was king.
Current economic models have not changed to address the new possibilities.

Behavioral Economics is for Kids!

Although I didn't recognize it at the time, I probably learned the basis of all global economic thought when I was twelve years old. Four of us twelve year old kids created an imaginary trading game where we all started with the same amount of imaginary money and a list of stocks and commodities and then we rolled the dice. A simple version of the game was that you picked a commodity like grain or gold or real estate, and then rolled two dice. One die indicated how many spots on the board you moved and the other die indicated whether it was a positive or negative move. If the second die was positive you moved to the right and made a profit. If the second die was negative, you moved to the left and made a loss. At the end of the game you would count up all the money each person had. The one with the most money won the game. So, depending on how the betting went, it was even possible to have less money than you started with but still win the game.

We all liked being with the other kids and it gave us something to do on rainy days, but eventually we began to lose interest, and stopped playing the game. I still wanted to play the game but I couldn't figure out what had happened to change our level of enthusiasm. And then I realized it. The over/under die was a simple plus/minus sign. It had a fifty percent chance of going up and a fifty percent chance of going down...Although I really liked it when my stock went up; I absolutely hated it when my stock went down. At the end of the game I always felt awful, even though fifty percent of my trades had gone up and fifty percent had gone down. The excruciating pain of losing money on my individual bad trades greatly outweighed the satisfaction of making money on my good trades. The overall feeling at the end of the game was frustration and pain. Since I expect we all felt the same way, we all stopped playing. After a period of time we all got together and came up with a solution. I believe that we came up with an idea that I believe has been at the center of every economic discussion since the time of the Romans.

What if we could rig the game so that all the bets were winners? It wouldn't change the eventual outcome of the game, in that there would still be only one winner. But instead of having some players on the plus side of the ledger and some on the negative side, we could ensure that everybody was on the plus side? Then everyone would be happy. So that is what we did. We eliminated the 'Plus/minus' die and said that all rolls of the die would be positive. The only question would be by how much. Instead of the pieces on the board going back and forth 'left and right' as you made or lost money on a trade, they would always go left to right as in a race, everybody moving forward, but at a different pace. The affect was amazing and immediate. The excruciating pain of a trading loss was gone, and the wins seemed even more exhilarating. The game was back on! We played for many more years under the new rules enjoying every minute. With that simple game we learned one of the biggest lessons of our economic careers. Emotions play a much larger role in economic thought and decisions than we had ever imagined.

Modern psychological study tends tells us that our brain is separate from our body and is capable of independent thought. So we always believe that our thoughts are unbiased and rational. However, in his book, "The Hour Between Dog and Wolf" John Coates (2012) shows us that the brain and the body are critically intertwined. And, since the large part of the brain, the neo-cortex, developed later in our evolution, the ancient parts of the spinal cord act like our primordial brain. Since these are mostly designed for "fight or flight" responses, they often react with strong emotions long before the neocortex knows what happened. Thus when, as kids our dice roles resulted in a loss, the negative feelings flooded our bodies before our brain could respond rationally. Eventually, we knew our decision to rig the game was irrational, but we did it anyways, and were much happier. Our emotions were in total control.

Every day, governments of the world make pretty much the same decision that we made over forty years ago as kids. We all know that the normal business cycle has ups and downs, good times and bad times. That is why they call it a cycle. However, if we could just rig the game so that every year was a good year, and we could eliminate the bad years, would we do it? Absolutely. This thinking has spawned a whole new field of behavioral economics.

The Destructive Power of 'The Leverage Cycle' .....Formerly known as 'The Business Cycle'

In many business text books, authors often pontificate on 'The Business Cycle', where business conditions improve, then deteriorate and then improve again in continuous cycles. Simple behavioral economics we learned as kids helps us to develop a more useful model, 'the leverage cycle'. At the start of this cycle, when everyone knows that business is getting better, people borrow money to buy assets that will go up in price (buildings, businesses, properties, etc.). The population is happy and politicians get re-elected. The money that was borrowed keeps the cycle going longer than it normally would and the value of assets escalates higher than they normally would. (ie. A bubble). When the rational business cycle turns down and the politicians want to get elected again, they adopt policies to artificially maintain or increase those asset values. So they drop interest rates and print money. That causes the prices of assets to go up and delays the onset of the down cycle.

In the case where the stimulus package cannot overcome the natural and eventual downturn of the business cycle, they crash much larger than anyone could have imagined. Then everyone says "Who knew?" Well in fact everyone knew it, they couldn't predict the actual timing, but they knew it and they didn't want to talk about it. That is when it becomes a 'leverage cycle'. Most of the value of the economy was based on the principle of leverage. It ends with massive de-leveraging.

The 10 Year Commodity Decline

One of the biggest stimulus periods of recent time was when three key 'historic' events came together at the same time creating the perfect storm for commodity prices and overall asset inflation. They were:

1. The U.S. Baby Boomers and the U.S. Housing Bubble
2. The formation of the Eurozone and the EURO currency
3. The rise of China as a global economic powerhouse

Any one of the three stimuli would have been a big boon for the world. But when they all came at once there was a stimulus beyond anything we could imagine. The global population, thinking this was normal however, borrowed throughout the first half of the cycle increasing leverage to unprecedented levels. Then came the crash of the U.S. housing market of 2007. This was the beginning of the end of the current business cycle. After that, Europe began to stagnate as the new Euro credit cards handed out to the participating countries began to run to their limits. Then China began to slow down as they could not continue to justify all the 'empty cities' and capacities that they had built. At the same time, all around the world people de-leveraged and commodity purchases slowed. We had been in a commodity boom cycle for twenty years, and now we were entering a commodity bust cycle of equivalent proportions. But like the kids we were, we assumed that this new elevated 'Hi-life' was the new normal and we didn't want it to end. So the U.S. and Europe entered the various phases of QE, 'quantitative easing' to try to stem the tide, while China reduced interest rates, tried to stimulate consumer purchasing and manipulate their stock market. All the central banks reached for their leverage levers. The ultimate question is..."Will the new artificial leveraging techniques be enough to overcome the de-leveraging of the previous unintentional leveraging?" If you can answer that, you can have an advance warning as to who will win the inflation game. Even if you can't answer that yet, you can see what a big effect leverage can have on the normal business cycle. The great investor Warren Buffet (2003) described 'financial derivatives' as weapons of mass financial destruction. Leverage can be considered a form of financial derivative. So when the business cycle turns into the leverage cycle, the outcome can become mass financial destruction.

The Problem with the Gold Standard

For centuries governments have wrestled with the same problem, how to spend more money on the voters than you physically have in the bank. The answer has always been the same, borrow more money. So when they wanted to buy votes, they borrowed money promising a lender that they will pay back the full amount, plus interest of course. But at some point when they had borrowed to their maximum limit, they had to pay it back. That was the problem. In the old days of the gold standard, this idea was pretty straightforward. The key attraction of gold as money was that it was in short supply. Very little new gold is found every year, so in reality you can consider the gold supply as fixed. If you borrowed a certain amount of gold, you had to pay back the same amount of gold. That was the problem with the gold standard. Over the centuries economies tended to grow when the government and its people borrowed the gold, but then contracted when they paid it back. The voters were ecstatic when new

26

infrastructure like new castles or aqueducts were built and jobs were created, but devastated when the gold had to be paid back and jobs were eliminated. Was there another solution?

Printing Money

The most predominant solution over the years was 'printing of money'. This has taken many forms, some brazen and some secretive. Most versions involve the development of a 'fiat or country currency', or a 'gold equivalent' currency that is supposed to be redeemable by the government for a predetermined weight of gold. Governments over time tell their constituents that this fiat currency is supposed to be a direct replacement for gold but will be used going forward because it is lighter or more durable, or easier to transport. Governments have said over the centuries that their specific fiat currency was developed and used instead of gold for the good of the country. "Long live our strong currency!" History tells us a different story. History tells us that, although these reasons are all true, the main reason countries develop fiat currencies is so that they can be duplicated and the value of each unit can be devalued as it relates to gold.

Anybody who watches old pirate movies can attest to this. Remember when the Spanish were dealing in the Caribbean and the currency was silver. Silver had similar benefits to gold in that it had a limited supply and was hard to duplicate. A single silver coin was called an eighth. This coin had a specific redeemable value. This coin could be cut into smaller pieces, called 'pieces of eight'. Do you remember what the first thing a pirate did when he was given a new coin? He bit into it to see if it was still pure silver or if it had been melted down and re-blended with softer lead. The harder the coin, the more silver was in it and the more valuable it was. Even at that time, the Spanish government was trying to make it's silver go farther. If you could take one silver coin and fabricate two, this would be a good way to pay back your debts. This was one of the original examples of money printing.

Since these early times, governments around the world have resorted to fiat currencies and money printing as a solution to the boom-bust business cycle. There is a whole school of economics dedicated to the printing of money called the Keynesian Theory Of Economics (Jahan, Mahmud, & Papageorgiou, 2014) that supports the printing of money. The theory is that when times are tough, the government should borrow/print money for infrastructure or other projects to get the economy moving and people employed. When times are good, the money should be paid back and the game gets back to neutral. The problem comes when the money is supposed to be paid back. The constituents get used to the new level of economic activity and wealth and see it as their 'god given right' to maintain that level. No government has the stomach to pay it back if there is a risk of not being re-elected, so the borrowing and the printing continues.

For example, for a given economy, let's assume that a normal level of unemployment is seven percent. However, with stimulus, government leaders determine that they can get unemployment down to six percent and get elected. After a few years the stimulus wears out and the unemployment goes to eight percent. All the constituents ask when is the unemployment rate going back to the normal six percent, which is a level that is unsustainable.

The Inflation Bias Propaganda

Governments have recognized over the centuries that the best way to get re-elected is to avoid the 'bust' part of the 'boom-bust' business cycle just as we did when we were kids playing our parlor game. Behavioral economics tells us that any anguish from the bust will be long remembered past the boom.

28

The best way to maintain the boom is by printing more pieces of your fiat currency.

The problem with this is that if you have the same amount of gold but hand out twice as many paper fiat pieces, eventually the value of the fiat currency will fall by half. So that items that cost one piece will eventually cost two. That is a simple example of inflation. If you only printed an extra ten percent of fiat currency, each unit would go down by approximately ten percent and it would look like goods and services went up by ten percent. In an extremely simplified world, printing ten percent more money would cause ten percent inflation.

The problem for governments is that, although this is the main reason why they want inflation, they are reluctant to say this in public in case people decide they won't accept the new fiat currencies. Fortunately, there are other valid reasons to create inflation, and governments have decided to focus on them.

Interestingly, the biggest reason that governments use to support inflation is that it is imperative that we avoid the deflation spiral. The simple logic is that people will put off buying things today if they believe that things will be cheaper in the future. If people don't continue to buy things today, that will slow down the economy and put more people out of work, increasingly in a vicious circle. This logic makes sense and is generally supported by the population. So much so that many governments actually publish an annual target rate for inflation. This target usually changes to meet the economic needs of the government of the time. At the time of this publication, inflation targets are generally in the range of two percent. But privately, governments want targets higher than the published rate, so that they can more easily pay off their debts.

One of the other benefits of high inflation is the fact that it tends to devalue your currency and make your exports more competitive. If you have twice as many paper fiat dollars in circulation as last year, but the same economic outlook, then your dollars are worth half and your currency should go down by fifty percent. I say should because it gets more complicated when you are dealing with multiple countries, each of which is trying to deflate their currencies. If two trading countries each devalue their currencies by fifty percent, then relatively speaking, they remain the same. So, in some cases it becomes a "race to the bottom".

Other benefits of creating inflation include being able to pay workers an ever-increasing wage, allowing retirees to earn interest on their bank accounts, and allowing governments to borrow incessantly and pay it back with an ever-devaluing currency. Of course much of this can just be illusory, just like in the old stock trading game. If inflation is five percent and you get a four percent wage increase or four percent interest at the bank, have you gained anything? No. In fact the new salary or interest is taxable. But somehow everyone goes along with the illusion. So the government makes more tax revenue by inflating the currency and we lose a little to the inflation rate each year. And, although never said publically, inflation has become the lifeblood of western governments. They thrive on it, they need it, they will perish without it. They will do everything they can to support it, and they will do everything they can to deny their addiction. They are trapped in a self degenerating circle of "spend and print".

So, as the whole global economic and financial infrastructure coalesces around the 'inflation forever' strategy, the global government mass marketing machine continues to pump out positive messages, financial forecasts and growth rates. They must keep the messaging positive to avoid mass panic. They keep talking about when things get back to normal. But what if they are wrong? What if this is the new normal? What will they do if inflation goes negative? What are we to do as individuals and as corporation?

When inflation goes negative, everything changes. But like any other major change, profits can go to those who are prepared.

Singularities, Swans, and Independent Thought

Another important reason for the existence of the 'Tin Foil Hat Society for Deflation' is paradoxically, because no one else is thinking about it. All the countries and economists are now singing from the same inflation song book. Until now our global economic history has taken a 'survival of the fittest' approach. Each country would take its own path and prosper accordingly. If they were on the wrong track they would fail and be taken over by an economy that was on a more effective economic strategy. There was no global central planning. It just worked out that the most efficient economic models survived and thrived while the others didn't. In 'The West and the Rest' Nial Ferguson (2011) describes with great detail the problem that arises if everyone has the same strategy. What if it's wrong? Who wins then? Or do we all lose collectively. What happens if we all proceed down the same economic path with the same economic assumptions until we hit a new unknown? This is what economists call a 'singularity' or a 'Black Swan' (Patterson, 2012). These are items that are supposed to be so rare that they are completely unpredictable. They are never supposed to happen. But they do happen, and they will happen more frequently.

In his book Dark Pools (2012), Scott Patterson describes the new generation of software trading programs and algorithms that have been developed using artificial intelligence and run independently inside the software trading venues of the NASDAQ and New York stock exchanges. Some of these trading programs are actually designed to develop their own mutant offspring and then measure their financial successes. If the new financial offspring are unsuccessful, they are destroyed. The successful offspring are allowed to mutate again thereby developing their own algorithmic ecosystem untethered to any programmer or company. When challenged by an SEC panel and a group of their peers, the developers all reluctantly agreed that they could not be absolutely sure what was going on within their new algorithmic eco-structure (Patterson, 2012). This is the perfect environment for a trading system singularity.

Knowing that our economic system is now measured in microseconds (one millionths of a second) I feel that we are more likely than ever to experience a singularity or black swan than we ever were before. I think it is more important now than ever before that we as individuals, governments and corporations allocate more resources to considering alternative economic scenarios and encouraging independent economic thought and discussion. Continuing to focus on the inflation scenario as the only outcome of our current economic efforts is irresponsible. When the world had multiple economic strategies in place we had choices. Now that we are all travelling down the same inflationary path, we have no back up plan. It had better be the right path.

Since 'inflation forever' is our current economic path we should be encouraging discussion, disagreement and stress testing. Then we need to explain those outcomes to the populace. What would happen if there were to be another bank failure? What would happen if the Eurozone experiment unraveled? How well would our system survive? Are there any other options? We need to let the population know the difficult choices we have in front of us. We can't keep them in the dark.

Lipstick On a Pig

Instead we are doing the exact opposite. Our economists and government officials keep denying that there is any problem. They keep talking about the future as being bright and shiny. They keep talking about 'when things get back to normal'. No matter how dismal the data becomes, they keep dressing the situation up to look good. Every country forecasts positive growth for the next year right up until it doesn't happen. Then they revise their forecasts down for the next six months, but up after that. We keep supporting the same economic system that got us into the situation we are in now. We need to look for other methods. They need to realize that at some point they need to be honest with the people in order to begin the process of finding ways forward.

Instead we keep finding short-term solutions to the problem by printing money globally and kicking the can down the road.

Chapter 2: New Paradigms for Deflation

Game Theory and Complex Systems

Part of the problem stems from the fact that the global economic system is quite complicated and extends across multiple scientific disciplines. On the one hand, countries can be modeled individually using traditional algebraic techniques like supply and demand. For instance, if the price goes down by ten percent, demand will go up by twelve percent. On the other hand global scenarios typically involve multiple human personalities and tend to follow more along the unpredictable laws of game theory. If I decide to devalue my currency by ten percent my exports should increase by twelve percent. But what happens if Japan sees what I am doing and retaliates by devaluing their currency? Do I get the desired effects on my exports or not? Probably not. With game theory, outcomes are not always linear. The outcomes are quite often 'either/or' solutions and can become quite unpredictable.

Complex Systems and Scenario Planning

Another factor adding to the difficulty is the fact that the global economy is a complex system. This means that not only is it complicated, but it is a learning system. It remembers what happened in the past and uses that information to decide on the future. So if I devalued my currency with no retaliation from other countries I may try this again later. However, other countries, having lost exports over that period, may retaliate differently this time. The same initiative as last time might have a completely different result this time. James Rickards (2011) describes exactly these types of scenarios in his book,

Currency Wars. Complex systems are continually redefining the rules of interaction and are therefore extremely hard to model and predict.

Quite often, modeling of these systems is made easier if you think of them as a game where a number of people are sitting around a table playing against each other. What will that person do next? The outcomes tend to be A or B type answers, not percentages. And the outcomes tend to be highly unpredictable the farther out and the more moves you try to predict. The best way to work with these types of systems is often scenario planning. In the real world, the number of possible outcomes can sometimes be unlimited and becomes too complex to work with. With scenario planning you try to work through the complexity by limiting the discussion to only a few possible scenarios, but working through each of those scenarios in great detail.

A good 'scenario planning session' should include a 'base case scenario' which should be the most probable scenario. This would be the basis for most of your business decisions. It should also include a 'best case' and a 'worst case' scenario. This would describe what would happen if everything went very well or very poorly. In addition, it should include three to five other alternative but realistic scenarios that would have a significant impact on the decision or business. Base case and worst case scenarios are easy to understand, but people quite often underestimate the usefulness of alternate scenarios. For example, what would happen to the global economic situation if shale gas discoveries in Europe lessened the need for natural gas from Russia. How would Russia react? Would they flood the market with more currency? Would they flood the market with their gold? Is our financial system designed to withstand a Russian retaliation? These would be good alternative scenarios to at least consider.

By the way, I am not suggesting that I have the answers to these questions. What I am proposing is that there be open discussion of the questions. Government economists and 'Think Tanks' should not go on blindly talking about the future of our inflationary world without at least talking about the possibility of a deflationary world. Deflation should be one of the alternate scenarios we discuss openly. And it should be one of the scenarios that we prepare for. Because when the water slows down, changes direction, and begins to flow upstream, none of our existing plumbing will work. It will be too late to begin talking about new pipes and pumps. Deflation can happen in an economic instant.

It's Not a Bubble - It's a Tower

In describing complex situations it is useful to describe things in visual terms. Economists have long discussed our current situation as an economic bubble. Central bankers keep pumping money and inflating this bubble. The bigger the bubble gets the more susceptible it is to bursting. John Mauldin (2011) describes our current economy as a 'bubble looking for a pin'. In his book, 'Endgame' he says that there are so many pins around the world today that it is difficult to predict which pin will finally pop the bubble, but one thing is for sure, the bubble is huge and the bubble will pop.

Although the bubble analogy is quite powerful, there is another analogy that adds a little more flare, and captures the emotional sense of risk. And that is the analogy of a tower. Imagine that the economic system of the world is like a tower being built up into the sky. Now imagine the S&P 500 as being one of those towers. At the time of this writing the S&P 500 was trading at around 2000, let's divide by ten and assume that the S&P 500 is a skyscraper reaching 200 stories high. Typical towers of the day range in the area of one hundred and twenty stories but advances in materials and building techniques have allowed towers to be safely increase in height by two to three floors per year. People are constantly clamoring for taller buildings.

The S&P tower is unique because it was built beyond traditional standards one floor at a time. Each time a new contractor added a floor on top and waited to see the result. The building would wobble but survive. The question is how much higher can it go? With each new floor comes a new risk. And when it comes down, will it be in an orderly fashion two or three floors at a time, or will it eventually collapse catastrophically under it's own weight? The bubble analogy implies a pop. The tower analogy includes risk, fear, and multiple demise scenarios. They both fit. I prefer the tower model.

The End Game - The Traditional Approach

Using the traditional approach, economists look back to the Great Depression of the 1930's trying to find clues. They publicly state that the depression was caused when the US Federal Reserve raised interest rates in 1933, precisely at the wrong time. However, they fail to mention the easy money policies of the prior decade and the fact that low interest rates were the actual cause of the bubble in the first place. The time to prevent the depression of the 1930's was in the decade of the 1920's.

We are currently in the same position as we were in 1933. To prevent a collapse into depression and the associated deflationary spiral, governments around the world are promoting a strategy of lowering interest rates close to zero and are printing money as fast as possible. In order for this to work, the governments of the world need to push the inflation story. People will borrow $100,000 at a 2 % interest rate to build a house if they think the value of their house will go up by 4 % per year. But they will not do the same if they think the value of the house will go down 4% per year. The governments have a vested interest in the inflation story.

How long can a bubble last? How high can a tower be built? The question of timing is a difficult one. John Mauldin (2011) says that "Things that don't make sense can go on longer than you think" (p. 204). Governments around the world are doing the best to delay the inevitable. So the timing is in question, but the direction is not.

Inflation - Deflation "Tug of War"

When most people think about inflation or deflation they think of a single identity and a single number. They talk about inflation being 'two and a half percent'. Although they may refer to different categories such as 'core' or 'non-core', typically inflation is treated as an absolute factor and an absolute number. In the understanding of inflation it is actually more helpful to think of inflation being divided into two separate forces, inflation and deflation. These two forces are in constant battle with each other. The concept of a tug of war is quite helpful, where the forces of inflation are constantly battling with the forces of deflation. The result of this tug of war is the actual inflation rate that we all talk about. So if the forces of inflation are pulling to the right at 5 percent, and the forces of deflation are pulling to the left at 3 percent, the net result is inflation (to the right) of 2 percent. The forces of inflation and deflation are battling each other all the time. The net result is the inflation rate. Inflationary forces tend to result when there is more demand for a product or service than there is supply. Prices tend to go up. Deflationary forces tend to occur when there is more supply than demand. Prices tend to go down.

The Freeze/Thaw Transition Line

When the rate of inflation changes but stays positive everything is fine. The problems come when the rate of inflation goes from positive to negative. That's where our administrative and financial systems have a huge problem; they are not designed for negative inflation. Interestingly, although the transition from positive to negative inflation is a big problem for us, it is not a problem for the economy. When thinking about this inflation/deflation threshold, it sometimes helps to talk about the weather.

Imagine a situation where it is a beautiful sunny afternoon. The air temperature is a balmy sixty-five degrees Fahrenheit. As the sun drops at dusk, the energy in the air drops and the air cools five degrees to sixty degrees. This five-degree of temperature drop is easily handled by the atmosphere and by us. No problem. Now imagine a different situation where the temperature is at thirty five degrees Farenheit and now the temperature drops the same five degrees. To the atmosphere, the five degree energy drop at thirty five degrees is approximately the same as the five degree energy drop at sixty five degrees. No big deal. For the atmosphere, there is nothing magic about thirty two degrees.

However, for us on the ground, everything changes. It's called freezing. All the rules that worked for "above freezing" conditions do not apply for "below freezing" conditions. Roads that supported cars easily during a rainstorm became a clogged mess below freezing. Tires that gripped the road above freezing need to be changed below freezing. Plumbing that worked perfectly fine above freezing cracks and heaves below freezing. That is just like inflation. It is very easy for the economy to move from inflation to deflation just like a drop in the temperature. And when inflation goes from plus five percent to three percent, it is not a problem. But when inflation goes from plus one percent to minus one percent, it is a big problem. Very few of our models that worked in inflationary times work in deflationary times. Does that mean that there is complete calamity and the end of the world? No. But it does mean that some things have to change. Knowing specifically what has to change and when to change it is the key to profiting from this inflation/deflation transition line.

Money Printing and M2..... useless models.

As I have mentioned before, models can either be a big help in understanding how things work or they can be a big impediment. Sometimes, models that were developed for a certain purpose continue to be used for other purposes, and completely obliterate the concept they are trying to help you understand. One such example is the money supply model called M2. Economists use it to describe the expansion and contraction of the money supply in a way to explain the business cycle. Then they use 'money printing' as a way to control it. Although these concepts are technically accurate, they don't help you to understand what is actually going on in the economy. Money printing is supposed to create inflation and get us out of our current problem. The U.S. Federal reserve has 'printed' unbelievable amounts of money. Why isn't it working? Because they are using a misleading model.

From an accounting point of view, the widely accepted model of money supply is called M2. The formula for M2 is the formula for how much money is in circulation. M2 = M1 times velocity. M1 is the amount of cash and cash equivalents around. Velocity is how fast it circulates in the economy. So, if there is lots of cash moving around then everything is great. So the two ways to improve the economy would be to increase the amount of money in circulation (print money) or to increase the velocity (move it around). The trick to a healthy economy is to get lots of money out there and make sure it turns over quickly. If 'the Fed' could print enough money, and I could spend it fast enough, things would be great. In talking to a number of my friends, we were all thinking of something like that. In fact while reading most economic forecasts, I think the pundits believe it as well. So why wasn't it working? The problem I had with this model was the term 'velocity'. What did that mean? In my mind I envisaged people taking in their paycheck and immediately going to a store to spend it. The faster we could all do that the better it would be for the economy. Obviously my model was wrong. To better understand what was really going on, I needed a new model. I needed a model that explained more intuitively to me what was actually happening.

'The Money Effect'......a better model.

Imagine a newly married couple living with one $50,000 income in a small home in a small mid-west town. After their family situation had stabilized they found that they could afford to go out for dinner one night per week and still maintain their standard of living. The economy was stable, and after a while they decided that they would like to go out two nights per week, but their income level couldn't support it. So they decided to borrow the money for the extra dinner by putting the cost of their second weekly night out on their credit card and not pay it back. After the first year they calculated that this extra dinner costs them $5000 per year. Many of their newlywed friends decided to do the same thing. To handle the new business, the restaurants in the area hired extra staff and a few new restaurants were built. The economy was booming. Prices were going up. So what happened here? Was the original model of M2 intuitively helpful? Was any extra money 'printed'? Not really. Were they spending any faster? No. Then what had really changed? Credit! That's what was missing from my model. Looking back into the formulas, I realized that economists included credit under the term velocity, but it hadn't really jumped out at me. So I came up with my own new version of M2 that specifically spelled out credit. Although not technically accurate, it went something like this:

M2 = (M1 x velocity) + 'Credit card debt'

Including the credit card in the equation changed everything. Including credit was like increasing their income by ten percent. It had a bigger effect that anything else they could do. It was clear to me that any model of the economy must include the impact of credit. To learn more, I went back to my scenario.

After five years of going out for dinner two nights per week, the credit card company phoned to say that couple had maxed out their credit card limit at $25,000 and the limit would not be increased. Knowing that they had to live within their means, the couple cut back on dinners to one night per week. So did their friends. The impact on the local economy was immediate. The restaurants began laying off people, and a few shut down. Construction jobs went away. And prices began to drop. What had changed here? The couple still had the same jobs as five years ago. They had the same income. Why were prices coming down? The only change was that they were now $25000 in debt. Then it hit me. It was not the level of the credit card debt the secret was the **change** in the level of credit. Increasing the level of credit was just like getting a raise. It had the same effect. So I came up with a new model of money called the "Money Effect", that included the **change** in the level of credit. The level of credit is sometimes called leverage.

'Money Effect M2' = (M1 x velocity) + '**change** in leverage'

So effectively, the economy could be affected by increasing the M1 money supply (printing money) or increasing the velocity (spending it faster) or by increasing the leverage. To learn what happened next, I went back to our small town.

As the couple expanded their credit, a funny thing happened. People came to believe that the high levels of growth, and employment were 'normal'. No one explained that this level of activity was only temporary until the credit line was maxed. All the people in the town made new plans based on this high level of activity. So what happened to the couple and the town when they had to cut back to levels of five years ago?

You can see from the example that even if the couple did not pay back the debt they ran up, the natural inclination of the economy in the small town would be to contract back to levels of 5 years ago. So the local government may try to help. The only thing they could do would be to forgive the loan that the couple took on. This is what people refer to as 'printing money'. This would actually cause M1 to increase. But would this help the economy? No. It would help to stabilize it, but until you can get the couple to increase their velocity of spending or take out another loan, simply printing money doesn't help. And which bank would lend them more money without previously securing a guarantee for the payment from the government?

And what would happen if the couple did try to be conscientious and pay off the bank loan? They would have to cancel their dinner out even one night per year (austerity). This means that the restaurants in town would lay off employees and close. This would cripple the economy and cause rampant deflation.

The Destructive Power of the "Leverage Cycle"

In our small town example you can see that increasing leverage caused the couple's spending to go up by 10% (from $50,000 per year to $55,000 per year). This was only intended to be a temporary phenomenon. However, over time, in everybody's mind $55,000 became the new normal. So when the couple maxed out their debt and cut back to one dinner per week, it felt like a 10% contraction in the economy. And when they began to pay back the loan over five years, it felt

44

like a 20 percent contraction. ($45,000 per year versus $55,000 at the spending peak 'normal'.) So, although mathematically you can see that everything is nice and tidy, from an emotional impact de-leveraging is a huge disruption. To the average person on the street, the growth side of the leveraging cycle feels good and becomes the new normal, while the de-leveraging side feels like depression. So we avoid it and don't talk about it. We run up huge deficits and then pretend they don't exist. Like the stock game of my youth, the anguish can be too much for our society to deal with. But you can see from our example that when we reach the max on our credit cards and can't borrow any more, (even if we don't pay down our debts), it will still feel like a recession. A good example of this is Japan where they built up their debt levels over twenty years and became a major powerhouse in the global economy. When they reached their maximum debt limit, their growth began to slow. So now, even though they have not paid anything back, they are in their second decade of slow growth, recession and deflation. So, the trick for us as a complex economy is to resist as much as possible the urge to use leverage now and pull forward projects which were planned for the future. We must resist this urge because we are fully aware of the huge pain and angst associated with de-leveraging later. Leverage is like a drug. The de-leveraging pain we feel later will be much greater than the leveraging pleasure we feel now. As mentioned earlier, I call this the "Money Effect". Leverage has a bigger impact on the economy than almost anything anyone else can do.

To illustrate this more graphically, I will use the following formula.

Money Effect M2:

Money Effect M2 = (M1 x velocity) + **change** in Leverage

Helicopter Ben (Bernanke)

When the change in leverage is zero (either at high or low levels of debt) the money effect M2 is equal to M1 times the velocity of money in circulation. You can increase the level of the economy and cause inflation in M2 by printing money (increasing the leverage.) If all the citizens are increasing their leverage at the same time that the government is increasing their leverage, then you can create a lot if inflation. The question has become, *Can the government print enough money to overcome a recession if all the citizens are de-leveraging*? The former Federal Reserve Board chairman Ben Bernanke always thought he could stop a recession just by printing enough money (Dorn, 2012). He was always famous for saying that the U.S. Central bank could cause inflation even if they had to drop money from a helicopter (Dorn, 2012). While he seemed to be correct for the United States so far, we have yet to see if the U.S. Central Bank can generate enough inflationary forces to overcome the massive deflationary forces currently throughout the world and win the 'global inflation-deflation tug of war'. That is the question.

Currency devaluation *is* Deflation

People tend to look at inflation from one side only, the side of the currency. If for example a loaf of bread goes from one dollar to two dollars, people think that the price has doubled and inflation is one hundred percent. The other way to look at it is as if you were the loaf of bread. Then you would say that, in bread terms the dollar has gone from one loaf to half a loaf. It has lost half it's value. The dollar has deflated by fifty percent. Since the second world war, people say that prices have gone up by a factor of twenty. A loaf of bread that was ten cents now costs two dollars. From the standpoint of the bread, the dollar has dropped in value by ninety five percent! It went from ten loaves per dollar to half a loaf per dollar. Why has this happened? Because politicians and central bankers would rather print money than pay our loans back. *To the bread this looks like massive currency devaluation. To us humans it looks like inflation.*

On the internet the other day I noticed something to the effect that people were expecting real estate prices to go up in the San Francisco Bay area once the Facebook shareholders were able to cash in their restricted stock options. I saw this as an interesting microcosm for international currency affairs. You can probably make the assumption that people as a group will always want more than they have. What limits us from getting it is money. If people have excess money, they would buy bigger cars, bigger homes, flashier clothing and vacations. Although there are individuals who are not like this, as a group I would argue that we humans are generally like this. What limits us is access to money.

The San Francisco scenario illustrates that if people have excess money they would begin to bid up housing prices until they could afford it no longer. Although it may take time, eventually they would bid up the prices until they were just as stretched as they were before the new money arrived. The situation appears to me to be that everyone is always going to be financially strapped to the max. The only question then becomes.... *What is the house price required to achieve this?* Now let's use this principle and go back to the board game.

Let's assume we are playing a simple game with five players. On the board of the game are five buildings. If each player had one dollar, what would the prices of the buildings be. Well they might fluctuate over time, but eventually they would settle around one dollar each. Now what happens if the government prints five new one dollar bills and gives an extra dollar to each player? Eventually the players would bid up the prices of the buildings to two dollars each, just like in San Francisco. So what happened to the price of the buildings. To the players, it appeared as though the buildings doubled in price (inflation). But to the buildings, it looked like the bank created new money by printing new bills thereby devaluing each bill.

If you assume that this is true, governments must have printed trillions of dollars over the past few decades on purpose, knowing exactly what would happen. They always express support for a "strong dollar". Why would they do this? Although they will never admit this publicly, they devalue the dollar purposely to avoid the excruciating pain of paying off their loans. If they can devalue the currency by half, they only have to pay back half the loan (half the number of loaves of bread). Currency devaluation is a powerful economic escape tool for governments who get into loan troubles. Sometimes they can use it to excess.

All Economies Naturally Deflate

Although we have experienced inflation almost non-stop for the last thirty years, inflation is not a natural phenomenon. It is a man-made creation. All things being equal, economies will deflate naturally. In absolute terms this means that productivity will improve and things will cost less. Given an economy where no new money is added, over time, people will tend to find ways to do things more efficiently. We classify these new processes and inventions as productivity improvements. Over the course of recorded time productivity improvements have come at different speeds. For example productivity would have increased dramatically after the invention of the wheel as many new inventions quickly followed. But productivity probably languished or even reversed during the centuries of the great plague. But typically, over the past thirty years people seem to think that productivity should reduce our costs by about two percent per year. Examples are all around us. Engines are going further on a tank of gas. Appliances are using less electricity. And homes are becoming more energy efficient. TV screens are getting bigger. All these advancements are increasing the quality of our lives and lowering our costs. In these cases deflation is affecting us all.

So if all economies naturally deflate, then why has there been so much inflation in the past thirty years? In the example above, notice that I said that if all things were equal. Well most of the time, all things are not equal. In the past few decades, while we have seen the traditionally deflationary forces, we have also seen major inflationary forces as well. One of the inflationary trends has been the growth in the number of baby boomers and family formation after the war. Everyone wanted new homes, cars, and appliances. Demand began to outstrip supply putting pressure on prices. Another has been the rise of locally manufactured and distributed products which caused the boomers to move out across the country. Another trend was the prosperity of the labor unions which forced costs up and spread the wealth across the country. Another trend that followed on was the growth of the global economy as countries increased their prosperity and began growing their own middle class.

Government Stimulus

When everybody talks stimulation to the U.S. economy they talk about helicopter Ben printing money. Recently, with his programs of quantitative easing, trillions of dollars were pumped into bond purchases to keep interest rates low and to stimulate the economy. In addition to this, the US government has also poured another $1.2 trillion per year of stimulation through government spending. The U.S. government spends about $3.6 trillion per year. When they announced permanent extension of the "Bush Tax Cuts", that meant that they only took in about $2.4 trillion per year in taxes. They effectively created a plan that would see them spend $1.2 trillion more than they took in taxes. That was like giving a $4,000 cheque to each citizen or $11,000 to each taxpayer, . (The other way of looking at this is that they were not collecting the $11,000 in additional taxes they would need from each taxpayer to cover their expenses.) One would think that between Ben Bernanke and President Obama, flooding the market with trillions of dollars in annual stimulus, this would certainly be enough to get the economy going and start the inflation ball rolling. But progress has been slow. Why has it taken so long?

I mentioned before that you can think of the annual rate of inflation as the winner of the 'tug of war' between the forces of inflation and the forces of deflation. With trillions of dollars of inflationary stimulus pumped in, here must be some serious deflationary forces in effect. What could they be?

Some of the major forces of deflation include the overbuilt US and international housing markets, the struggling European economic situation, and the emerging sluggish global demographic trends. A recent speech given by author and newsletter writer Harry Dent (20012) was called "A decade of Volatility: Demographics, Debt, and Deflation." In it he says, "There is simply no way the Fed can win the battle it's currently waging against deflation, because there are 76 million baby boomers who increasingly want to save, not spend. Old people don't buy houses!".

He explains in *The Great Depression Ahead* (2009) that the peak of the recent housing boom featured upper-middle-classed families living in 4000 square foot McMansions. "About ten years from now," he says, "what will they do? They'll downsize to a 2000 square foot townhouse. What do they need all those bedrooms for? The kids are gone. They don't visit any more. Ten years after that. Where are they? They're in 200 square foot nursing homes. Ten years later, where are they? They're in a 20 square foot grave plot. That's the future of real estate. That's why real estate has not bounced in Japan after 21 years. That's why it won't bounce in the U.S. either. For every young couple that gets married and has babies, and buys a house, there's an older couple that is moving into a nursing home or dying."

The baby boomers ended their peak spending years in 2007 and goes on to say that painful chronic deflation will be here for quite some time.

The New Inflation Equation

To say that there is no mathematical equation that explains all this is an understatement. In fact there is not even universal agreement on what all the key factors are. Does this mean that we stop here? No, it just means that we build, from first principles, with the pieces we know to be true. So far we have been dealing with a rough cut formula for M2. Let's modify it and see if we can use that as a basis of our inflation equation. We know that inflation is equal to the sum of all the inflation forces and all the deflation forces. So let's try the equation below:

$$\text{NET INFLATION} = \frac{\text{MONEY PRINTING}}{\text{GOVT STIMULUS}} - \begin{array}{l}\text{OVERBUILT HOUSING}\\ \text{GLOBAL DE-LEVERAGING}\\ \text{GLOBAL DEMOGRAPHICS}\\ \text{PRODUCTIVITY IMPOV.}\end{array}$$

Since our economies are now linked internationally, each country can do its part, but the real question is: 'Will the global government programs of money printing and stimulus be enough to overcome the existing global deflationary forces?' It appears for the bankers around the world that a helicopter will not be enough to spread the money. Perhaps they will need flying aircraft carriers pouring cash out of thirty six inch pipes all across the country. The scope of the deflationary forces may be too big to overcome, or the price that we may have to pay could be too steep.

…and this is before we fully understand the greatest deflator of them all the internet.

The Internet -- The Great Deflator

Have you heard any economist around the world talk about the internet as the greatest deflation tool ever created? Have you ever wondered why?

 As Michael Porter (2008) described in his book, *Competitive Strategy, Techniques for Analyzing Industries and Competitors* one of the biggest factors in determining the profits of a market is the number of competitors in that market. He calls the number N. When the number of competitors in a market is small, profits tend to be higher, such as a monopoly or oligopoly (Porter, 2008). And that is true for all the suppliers and other members of the value chain. As the number of competitors goes up, the profits for everybody go down. The classic example is the case of the monopoly where this little pressure on prices or profits. But let's look at what happens when the number of competitors goes up over time.

Let's go back to our small town. And let's assume that I am the only building contractor in that town. Every time someone wants to put up a building they must go through me. Customers know they are paying a premium, but want quality and they want their project done on time. I pretty much control the market and the prices. All my suppliers are well taken care of and realize that they must tow the line. Now let's assume that a new contractor comes to town and starts to win some projects. My business suffers a bit, and I lose a little control of my supplier base, but I am able to meet my competitor at conferences and come to some understandings. A few months later, another contractor comes to town and we have a similar conversation. Everything is still ok, but I am finding that I am only winning one in three contracts now, and my costs are staying the same. This has resulted in my profits going down. Then two more contractors come to town and I tend to start losing control. I am only winning one in five contracts. I start to lose influence in the market I once controlled.

When the sixth competitor comes in to town, my focus turns to winning the next job and cost control. I have slowly been dropping my prices but I have not won a job in a while. I must now take drastic action. So I go to the customer and redesign his building to reduce costs, I redesign my work flows and reduce staffing levels to reduce costs, and I pressure my suppliers to reduce costs. Occasionally I go directly to offshore suppliers directly to reduce costs. My competitors do the same, and all my suppliers do the same. As the number of competitors goes up, the whole value chain tends to focus on productivity improvement, quality improvement, and cost reduction. And this is not a one time change. This is a permanent change in the value chain eco system as long as the number of competitors remains high.

So how does the internet affect this? The internet permanently increases the number of competitors, N. In your small town there may have been two or three competitors supplying a product or service and making a nice financial return at a reasonable price.
With the internet, there can now be an infinite number of competitors. New low cost competitors can emerge across the street or across the ocean. They can be large conglomerates or individual proprietors. Product or engineering files can be emailed or shipped overnight across continents. Customer service calls can be handled in other countries. Everyone's quality is going up. Everyone is a competitor. The number N goes to infinity. Fewer and fewer products and services can avoid the impact of the internet. There will remain a few

pockets of protection like biogen or medicine where companies will be protected by proprietary information or patents, but everyone else will be hurled into the internet deflationary spiral. The internet may be the greatest deflationary productivity tool in our history. The future impact of the internet on deflation will be astounding. Try to remember, this is not a bad thing. It is a good thing. *(....keep your tin foil hat on......)*

When you re-write our inflation equation with the internet deflation factor included, it might look like this:

$$\text{NET INFLATION} = \frac{\text{MONEY PRINTING}}{\text{GOVT STIMULUS}} - \frac{\text{OVERBUILT HOUSING}}{\substack{\text{GLOBAL DE-LEVERAGING} \\ \text{GLOBAL DEMOGRAPHICS} \\ \textit{INTERNET DEFLATOR}}}$$

If the internet deflation factor is as large and permanent as it appears to be, there may be no way that the governments can counteract this pull in their global tug of war. No one can say for sure what the absolute mathematical relationships are between all these factors, ie. what are the multipliers or ratios. In fact just agreeing that these are the key factors would be a great achievement. However, if this inflation equation is anywhere close to reality, then deflation will become the new normal. We must all figure out how to deal with it.

Current Productivity Measures Don't Apply
........We need the New: 'UBER Math'

A good example of the deflating power of the internet is with the Uber taxi service. In this case the person in need of a ride simply logs on to his or her phone and requests a driver. One of many local drivers immediately replies with his approximate response time. In the traditional taxi approach, the rider typically had access to a small number of service providers in a certain geographic area. In the new Uber approach, hundreds of riders have access to hundreds of drivers in a given area. Using Michael Porter's (2008) logic, the number (N) of competitors (drivers) goes from three or four to one hundred or more. And remember, as the number N goes up, the costs typically go down. So the user sees a big increase in service at a lower cost. This disruptive kind of approach is good for the new drivers, but bad for the traditional taxi companies.

Now here is another problem. Except for traditional taxi drivers, everyone I talk to thinks that Uber service increases productivity. If two people decide to go to a restaurant, they can contact an Uber driver who will respond in less time for less cost. I call that a great productivity improvement. However, if you look at our traditional productivity measurements, it would indicate the opposite. The traditional calculation for productivity is 'output dollars divided by input dollars'. This calculation works in an inflationary world but not in a deflationary world.

By way of an example, let's assume that the taxi service would cost $40 and the Uber service would cost $30. (This is an example of good deflation.) Let's also assume that both services take an hour to complete and both services cost $20 to complete. The traditional approach to productivity measurement would indicate that the taxi service was more productive at a 2/1 ratio while the Uber service was less productive at a 1.5/1 ratio. While this is true mathematically, it doesn't feel right. From a user standpoint, it feels like the Uber service is a productivity enhancement, not a detractor. The problem with this old method is that it does not take into account the possibility that the numerator (the revenue) can go down. It always assumes inflation. In the new deflationary world, when the revenue number goes down, it improperly skews the calculation. I expect that economists will be distressed when they see productivity decreases around the world, when in fact they are seeing productivity gains through deflation. Do I have the answer today? No. But I do see the problem. I think we need a new calculation….a new Uber calculation. When the water goes backwards, all the plumbing needs to be looked at.

How to Survive and Prosper In the Deflationary Spiral

Once people begin to believe that life with deflation is a possible scenario, they come to fear the 'Deflationary Spiral'. In this scenario, prices stop inflating and eventually begin to drop. But as people begin to understand that things will be cheaper in the future, they start to put off purchases. As they begin to put off purchases, demand declines and prices spiral lower. At first this appears to be a positive thing as items begin to be cheaper. But then your company begins to have price pressures and your wages begin to fall as well, either through wage reduction or layoff. Once you understand that your wages will start to go down, you will be more hesitant to purchase unnecessary items. Once the market understands that deflation is permanent, there is no urgency to buy big ticket items. This is especially true when you go to buy a house. Why would you buy a house when you know that the price will go down in five years, but the loan you have will retain its value?

Taking out any kind of a loan in a deflationary world is not advised. You would be smarter to be a lender. It will become much more difficult for a family to buy a car, or start a family. Now consider what this same realization does to a whole country after ten years, and you will see why many people want to avoid it. This has been the situation in Japan for many years.

Japan: A Decade of Deflation

Japan has been vacillating between inflation and deflation for over a decade. In 2014 deflation was winning the tug-of-war. The deflation bell curve was in full view with recreation and clothing down about one percent, education down around 13 percent and furniture down approximately three percent. This is taking its toll on the Japanese people. Just as inflation has made a big imprint on our outlook, deflation is changing the expectations of the Japanese people.

A new sense of resignation has enveloped that nation. Twenty years ago Japan was a nation of pride and energy. Today, deflation has left a feeling of pessimism and resignation. The changing outlook can be seen in Tokyo where the large number of 'Micro-houses' have become popular with younger people who can't afford traditional living quarters. These small homes are built on tiny plots and have tiny apartments with micro-sized kitchens. Some of these properties include studios and shared social areas.
They are designed for young people who can't afford a home, or are unsure of the future.

The issue now is that the Japanese are getting accustomed to the situation and are expecting prices to deflate. This has become a generational problem as well. In some instances, deflation is causing the Japanese population to hoard their wealth. They have become reluctant to share their accumulated wealth until they die. The result is that the Japanese, who have one of the longest lifespans in the world, are not receiving their inheritance from their parents until they are in their sixties, well beyond the major spending years. This is causing a large amount of wealth to sit idle, thus lowering the velocity of money even more. Japan has been in and out of a deflationary spiral for the past decade and has recently devalued their currency as the only escape route. This has resulted in some good progress on a local currency basis.

However, as will be discussed shortly, if you take into account the recent devaluation of the yen versus the U.S. dollar they are still in the quagmire.

The 'Inflation - Deflation Bell Curve'

The key to profiting from deflation is in the understanding that not all items inflate or deflate at the same speed. Some items are deflating while others are inflating. The usual measure of inflation is the Consumer Price Index, commonly known as the CPI. This CPI represents a basket of goods and services that are supposed to represent a good cross sampling of things we buy.

There are two basic types of data needed to construct the CPI: price data and weighting data. The price data are collected for a sample of goods and services from a sample of sales outlets in a sample of locations for a sample of times. The weighting data are estimates of the shares of the different types of expenditure in the total expenditure covered by the index. In 2015, the weights were as follows: Housing: 41.4%, Food and Beverage: 17.4%, Transport: 17.0%, Medical Care: 6.9%, Other: 6.9%, Apparel: 6.0%, Entertainment: 4.4%

Two things come to mind here. The first is that I have my own personal inflation rate since I consume categories at a different rate than someone else. For example as I age, maybe my medical care costs go up and my housing costs go down. Secondly, not all these categories are going up or down at the same rates.

Although the government states that our current inflation rate is about 1.5%, that is just the average. Many items are already in a deflationary position. Consider the cost of flat screen TV's.

They are deflating at a rate of about 20% per year and keep increasing in quality. Also consider the publishing industry where e-readers are pushing the cost of books down drastically and on-line advertising is pushing newspapers almost to the point of extinction. Although our overall inflation rate may average 1.5 %, many industries are deflating rapidly.

Of course that means that many industries are still inflating. The cost of, medical care, education and many other services are increasing. To get a better understanding of this phenomenon it could be helpful to place them on a chart with the biggest deflators on the left and the biggest inflators on the right. The most likely distribution would be similar to a "bell curve" with a few outliers on the left and right, but most items in the middle. The middle would be right around 1.5% inflation which would be the published rate.

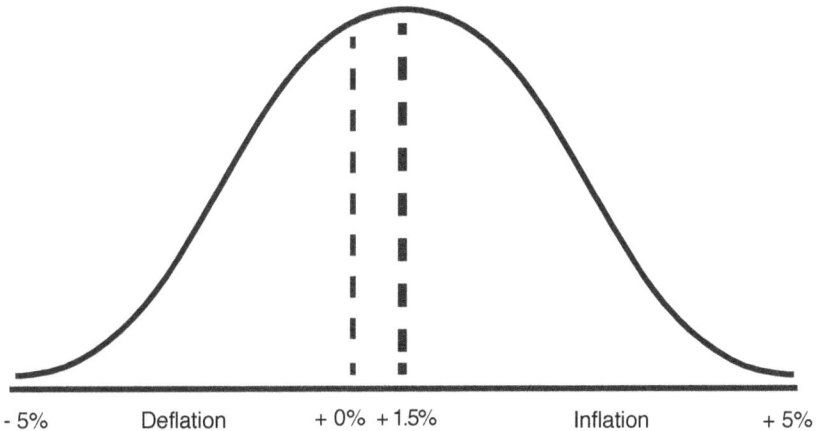

| - 5% | Deflation | + 0% + 1.5% | Inflation | + 5% |

What you can see from this type of chart is that while we are still experiencing overall inflation, about 40 % of the items are actually deflating. And if the chart moves just a little to the left, and inflation goes to zero, then 50 % of the items will be inflating while 50% will be deflating. Understanding what is inflating and what is deflating and predicting whether that chart will move left or right is the secret to making money during periods of deflation. The simple answer is to invest in assets that are inflating and not in those that are deflating. But the world is a complex place that responds and learns. People and countries react and retaliate. Nothing stays the same. The secret lies in predicting what happens next. For that we will need another model.

The U.S. Dollar is the only Global Scoreboard

Because of its long and significant history around the globe, the U.S. dollar is the de facto currency of the world. Most commodities (oil, gold, copper etc.) and most other currencies are valued against it. It is the basis for most global transactions. Therefore, all discussions of deflation must be measured in U.S. dollars.

This is important because currency devaluation is another form of deflation. If you are working in a country outside of the United States, you may not be able to change the currency of your paycheck, but you can put all your other investments into U.S. dollars. So all global investors should think of things in U.S. dollars. It is the only true reference point, the only global scoreboard.

So, if you work in France, and the Euro loses ten percent against the U.S. dollar, your country would have experienced ten percent deflation. The cost of your labor has declined ten percent. If you live in a commodity exporting country you are almost certain to experience deflation as we work through the commodity bust cycle.

Even though the concept of the global scoreboard sounds simple, the world fails to grasp it. In fact global economists build currency devaluation into their inflation models that is fed to the masses. This is misleading. Consider a simple situation. Suppose your currency devalues by ten percent. You would see a portion of the things you buy go up in price by ten percent. If thirty percent of the things you buy go up by ten percent, you may experience three percent inflation in local currency. However, this is not actually the case. If you look at it in terms of U.S. Dollars, you would have experienced seven percent deflation. If an international employee takes his paycheck and immediately puts it into U.S. dollars, he would have experienced seven percent deflation, not three percent inflation. That is the truth. That is the way global investors look at the world.

As simple as this concept sounds, most international inflation/deflation models do not take this into consideration and are therefore misguiding the local population. The first rule of global investing should be to ask how this looks in terms of the U.S. dollar. All other decisions should be made in this light.

Deflation Wars ! - The Exporting of Global Deflation (In U.S. Dollars)

All the countries of the world report inflation in local currency. In local currency most countries are operating in the zero to plus two percent range. I think this is extremely misleading since it only tells part of the story. When you report the same data in terms of constant U.S. dollars, many countries, especially commodity countries, are deflating at ten to twenty percent per year! What a large difference! Why isn't anybody talking about this? What would the populations do if the government published data like that? There would probably be a mass exodus of money into U.S. dollars.

When the economy slows down, countries have always tried to deflate their currencies in order to help their exports at the expense of the other countries. This also causes imports to look more expensive and causes inflation in local currency. This tactic has come to be known as 'Currency Wars. In reality they do this via lower interest rates, so you could think of this as 'lower interest rate wars'. And, if you take this idea to the extreme, you develop the concept of 'Deflation Wars'. As the global economy slows, countries will lower their interest rates to devalue their currency trying to 'import inflation and deport deflation'. The only way to make this deceitful plan work is for local governments to keep track of inflation in local currencies. If you keep your statistics in terms of U.S. dollars it would be obvious what was happening and the population may revolt.

'Global In-deflation' a Simple but Powerful Concept

Many of the economic headlines we see around the world quite often seem to be contradictory or don't make sense to us. This is because of two reasons. The first reason is that there is simply no English word that accurately describes inflation-deflation as a continuum. Typically inflation and deflation are described as two different things rather than just different manifestations of the same phenomenon. This adds unnecessary complexity to the situation. For example, if we want to know a bit about the weather outside, we will ask *What's the temperature outside?* We don't ask *What is the positive temperature?* or *What is the negative temperature?* We just ask *What is the temperature?* Similarly on the inflation front, we need a word that more accurately depicts what is actually happening. I will refer to this as the '*In-deflation*' number. It is quite reasonable for this number to be positive or negative. This simple concept automatically suggests that inflation and deflation are different manifestations of the same concept. Both are not only possible but are quite acceptable. It removes the 'deflation stigma' from the conversation. You might more accurately ask *What is the in-deflation number for that country or product?* For Germany the correct in-deflation number might be plus two. For Italy it might be minus one. Asking for the in-deflation number recognizes the fact that things can and will go either way. If you ask for the inflation rate, that assumes it can only go one way. And, I am also suggesting that, in the future, lower costs might suggest high productivity and deflation, and that's a good thing. In the future, a deflating economy might be a badge of honor, not a symbol of failure. It might become a symbol of efficiencies and prosperity, not as a failure. As simple as that sounds, I believe this is true. A simple word or phrase can make a huge difference. If you put your sunglasses on it is easy to see.

The second reason deflation seems so hard understand is that we tend to think about things from our own country status. That has to change. As stated previously, the U.S. dollar is the global currency. Each country must therefore relate their situation using the United States as a reference point when they talk about inflation. Consider an example where Canada and the United States are running along in parallel. They may have the same interest rates and unemployment rates and growth rates. Then for some reason Canada starts to grow faster. Why could that be? To the casual observer, that does not appear to make sense. The problem is that the newspaper headlines we read tend to look at situations in isolation. The headline might say "Canadian economy now growing faster that U.S." However, when you look further you might find that Canada has lowered their interest rates, and therefore their dollar, and therefore their exports begin to grow. Now that story makes sense. (But it is too long for a headline.) If the Canadian dollar stayed at par with the U.S. dollar, Canada would not have grown faster. However, having reduced their dollar by twenty percent their growth in local currency has gone up five percent, it now begins to make sense. However, is it worth it? Once you look at the full story in U. S. dollars, Canada is still fifteen percent behind.

As a result of high speed computing, the internet, and international finance, each local economy can only be understood from a global perspective. Once you use the right model to look at each local situation, just like in our basketball example, the answers will become more clear. So if you put the concept of 'In-deflation' together with the concept of the global (U.S. dollar) view, you come up with a concept of *'Global In-deflation'*. Now, if you look at the world and your local market, through your global in-deflation sunglasses, things will come into focus.

Chapter 3: Visions of the Future

Virtual Real Estate Deflation

The old saying that 'Information wants to be free' is now starting to have a huge impact on economic thought. More and more of the things we consume are virtual. Remember when we used to get in our car and 'go for a drive'. Remember when our kids used to go outside and play with the new sports equipment we bought them. Remember when we used to buy books or go out to movies.

We still need food and clothing, but we don't consume as many of the other physical things as we used to. Many of the things we do now are virtual. We download movies, or books, or music. We play video games or talk on Skype. For many of us, one of our biggest expenses now is our internet, cable and mobile phone bills. The world is going virtual, and it is going mobile.

In some major cities housing costs gone so high that they have gotten out of reach for many young people, so they don't even think of home ownership. They want to travel, and be with their friends. At one point I asked a young millennial if she was saving to buy a home she said, "You don't get it do you. My generation doesn't want homes. We want to travel and see the world with friends. Do you know where my home is?" Then she held up her phone and pointed to the apps. "Here it is", she said. "This is my home, and these are my rooms, and this is where my friends live. Unlike you, my friends travel with me all the time. I have a virtual house that fits in my purse. It has one hundred rooms. How do you like it? What would you rather have?"

Your Personal Deflation Rate   ('Prescription' Sunglasses)

Well she had a point that agreed with Harry Dent. In 25 years I will have my own 25 square foot patch of real estate. What do I need a house for? I need a smaller place closer to my friends. That might, in fact, reduce my costs of "Housing" as stated in the CPI calculations. As I began to think about it I realized that I might have a deflation rate that was different from the next person because of my position in my life. As I grow older I will tend to consume more things virtually than physically. And the virtual things in life are generally becoming much cheaper. If I was younger I might be increasing my consumption of physical goods that may be still inflating.   In looking at the bell curve, the only thing that I see that is on the right side of the curve for me and that I will consume more of in the future is medical services. And that it such a major topic, I believes it needs separate discussion. So, except for medical services, I believe all my costs will eventually move from right to left on the deflation curve, thereby lowering my costs each year. Everyone is different. Depending on where you position yourself on the curve will help you determine your personal estimated future deflation rate. if the overall inflation rate was 5%, you may be able to move yourself to 2% to 3%. However with average inflation around 1.5%, you may be able to improve your financial position by moving yourself into a 1 or 2 % deflationary cost spiral. To do this you must understand that both inflation and deflation are just different ends of the same phenomenon. You need to feel comfortable moving up and down the chart.

Salaries and Wages in Deflationary Times

There has always been the question, *What comes first, deflation or lower salaries?* I believe the answer lies in the business cycle. During the expansion phase jobs and wages grow. Towards the end of the cycle the government wants to extend it so they print money. However at some point the declining cycle overwhelms the expansive printing and we enter a downturn bigger than if we hadn't printed all that money. At that point salaries don't go down per se. What happens is that people lose their jobs and get hired at a later date into a lower paying job. When this happens the number of people with jobs increase and unemployment goes down, but since the jobs are lower paying, the total wages paid to employees goes down. It is the wages number that drives the economy, not the jobless rate. During deflationary times the objective is try to find work in an expanding field that cannot be done offshore and to keep your job at the same pay rate, and rent don't buy, whenever possible and watch the world as most other things get cheaper.

Food Costs - the great Unknown

It is possible that wages will go down faster than deflation. In this situation people will have to make choices. People will cut back on luxuries, but splurge in small ways to keep up their disposition. They will be forced to make choices. One of the choices they will make will be food. Over time food will become a larger part of their household expenses. They will treat themselves to more expensive specialty items from time to time, but eventually they will have to cut back in other areas. As a result, food may be the slowest item to deflate. If you invest in anything, the food chain may be the best opportunity.

Saudi Oil – *Pump! Pump! Pump!*

---- *What Would I do if Oil and Gas Were Free?*

When I was young, gasoline was selling for thirty nine cents per gallon. Globally it was trading from two dollars to ten dollars per barrel. Most of it came from Saudi Arabia since they had the lowest costs in the world. Then, over the years, the Saudi's figured out that people would pay almost anything for their petroleum, so they began to increase the price. As the prices went up, people still bought the oil but they found that other countries also began to produce it. Saudi oil began to lose influence, and pricing became erratic, so the Saudi's formed a cartel of oil producing countries in order to keep prices up.

This oil producing cartel called OPEC, worked for many years eventually raising the price of oil above one hundred dollars per barrel until 2014 when lower cost 'oil fracking technology' engulfed the United States. The fracking companies (frackers) could get oil out of the ground at a cost of fifty to sixty dollars per barrel. When the selling prices were over one hundred dollars per barrel, they were making large amounts of money and flooding the markets with oil. People maybe haven't realized it yet, but these frackers have changed everything forever. For decades the Saudi's have resisted dropping their prices. But fracking technology was 'the straw that broke the camel's back'. (Pun intended). The Saudi's realized that, in order to maintain their leadership role in the market, they would have to change their strategy and reduce their prices.

All the pundits that I have talked to say that the Saudi's wont decrease their prices because, although it may only cost them ten dollars to produce a barrel of oil, they need 'Ninety dollar oil' to support their social programs and their economy. Again, that is true under the old paradigm. What if there were a new way at looking at oil prices.

Sometimes, when I come to a strategic juncture in game theory like this, I drop all the economic equations and wonder if there is a new possibility. I use game theory. I think *What would I do if I were the King of Saudia Arabia?*

Well, if I were the king of Saudi Arabia and I knew I had the lowest cost oil in the world… I think I would pump oil until the pipes began to burst. And then I would build more pipes! In a simplified world, if oil is selling for fifty dollars per barrel I need to sell twice as much as I do at one hundred dollars per barrel to get the same amount of money into my coffers to feed my people. No problem! What good is oil doing me if it is sitting in the ground? If I have a two hundred year supply in the ground and I double my pumping capacity I will only have a one hundred year supply left. Who cares? No one cares. This concept goes against economic theory, but fits right into game theory. As the King, if I double my capacity I will reduce the prices. But I will own the market again, regain my lost influence, feed my people, and no one will know the difference. They won't know the difference for 100 years! I want results now. So, what would I do? PUMP! That's what I would do "if I were King of Saudi Arabia". I would say to the frackers "Don't show me your textbooks. Show me your oil. Oops you have none at twenty dollars per barrel. So Sorry! Good bye." That's what I would say to all my global competitors with higher variable costs. I would put them out of business and control the world oil supply again. I would show the world that Saudi Arabia is truly the world's only oil superpower. Sometimes economics doesn't follow economic theory, it reverts back to the basics of game theory. This is one of those cases.

How low can the price of oil go? And how will it affect the world? I don't have all the answers, but I do have a unique way to approach the problem. In extremely disruptive economic situations like this I find it helps if I go immediately to the extreme and ask myself a question like....*What would I do if oil and gas were free*? I am asking myself that question right now. That question will be sure to add a number of possible scenarios to your planning exercise. Good 'fuel for thought'.

So, if you see Saudi Arabia building up their oil producing infrastructure in the future, don't listen to what they say, look at what they are doing. Prepare yourself. "So sorry".

The Case for Lower Interest Rates

I started the discussion of this book with a mental image of inflation, negative interest rates, and water flowing in the wrong direction backing up the plumbing. At that point these ideas probably seemed quite foreign and implausible. That's because the government absolutely doesn't want deflation, and doesn't even want anyone to even think about the possibility. They are desperately afraid that any discussions will become a self-fulfilling prophesy. So they purposely keep the discussion focused on inflation. However deflation is currently occurring in many areas of the economy and is only one 'central bank mistake' away from spreading to other sectors. The same is true with interest rates.

The only real tools available to the government are monetary and fiscal stimulus. Monetary stimulus means interest rates and fiscal means tax and spend. (Or more accurately spend and then don't tax enough). All the governments realize that they are in a dangerous period of global de-leveraging and that we will enter a period of dangerous deflation like Japan unless they pull out all the stops. They don't know exactly how much stimulus they need, but they would rather err on the side of too much rather than not enough. On the monetary side this means that governments lower interest rates as low as possible. This has a two pronged affect. Not only does it attempt to encourage borrowing, but it lowers the government's cost on the huge debts that it has already incurred. Governments will try to keep interest rates as low as possible for as long as possible because if interest rates were allowed to rise, the higher borrowing costs would cripple the government itself. There has been a keen global push to continually lower interest rates. But how low can they go?

Negative Interest Rates: 'Embrace and Enhance!'

People always talk about when interest rates 'return to normal'. Well, what is normal? Normal is the interest rate that the government feels best meets its needs at the current time. Sometimes that means high interest rates, other times low interest rates. Typically, if you put your money in the bank you expect to receive an interest rate that is above the rate of inflation. So if inflation was three percent, you may expect to achieve four percent interest. But what if the government wanted you to go out and spend your money. They might lower bank interest rates to two percent. So if the value of a new commercial building was increasing by three percent per year, you might go ahead buy the building with money borrowed at two percent and make a nice profit of one percent per year for twenty years. However if interest rates were four percent, you would not make that same investment because you would lose one percent per year. If interest rates fall below the rate of inflation, they are said to be 'negative real interest rates'. So even though you may have actual positive interest rates, it is possible to have negative real interest rates at the same time. That is a very important distinction.

Currently some countries are talking about ever lower interest rates or negative rates, while other countries are talking about raising their interest rates. As I mentioned before it is possible for countries to have different in-deflation rates, and therefore different interest rate strategies. But they are all interconnected in the global economy. In August of 2012 yields on the two year Euro bonds were .05 percent. That's not half a percent, that's one twentieth of a percent. Mario Draghi, president of the European Central Bank did not want European banks storing money in his central bank. If you assume that inflation was 1.5% at the time, people who did store their money there were losing 1.45% to inflation. That was 1.45% of real money. When interest rates are below the inflation rate you have negative "real interest" rates. People will borrow money from the bank and let inflation do the work. Even though the interest rate is positive, it is less than inflation, and you make money. This is a "Negative real interest rate". However implausible it may seem, once you come to accept the reality of negative "real" interest rates, a full move to negative interest rates is not too far behind.

The problem is with inflation rates at 1 or 1.5% percent is that there is not much room for error. If you make the assumption that the central banks are lowering rates to get you to move your money around, what happens if they get interest rates to 0% and the economy is still not moving? Perhaps we can go back to Japan where Prime Minister Shinzo Abe said that he wants the Bank of Japan to set interest rates at zero or below zero to enhance lending and lower the value of the Yen to enhance exports. This means that ordinary people would either earn no interest on their money or have to pay for storage on their money. Although this seems absolutely foreign to us, it would make sense for a Japanese investor if they could store their money at a cost of 1 percent and deflation was 2 percent. Although they would be losing money on an absolute basis, the real financial return for them would be positive. This need not be a frightening concept to us. If understood correctly, it can be a great wealth generator. In his book *The Road Ahead* (1995) Bill Gates explains that we must embrace the internet and enhance it. I believe we must embrace and enhance deflation.

The " I.O.U. Bank" - A Killer App for Big Data!

Imagine that deflation is running at four percent. That means that things would cost four percent less one year from now. Another way to view the situation would be to say that your money would be worth four percent more one year from now. So, if you were to sell something and the buyer paid you one year from now, they would actually be paying you four percent more than the actual cost of the product or service. As a result of this phenomenon, you would probably start asking your customers to pay you later. In the extreme case you could probably reduce your current price slightly, but you would not allow them pay you for at least a year. Further to this, at the end of the year, if they were credit worthy, you might ask them not to pay you for another year. In fact you might just "roll over" all your receivables and ask to never get paid. You would be making 4% on your receivables. We would quickly move from a 'cashless society' to a 'payment-less society'. Your receivables would be a collection of 'I.O.U. s to infinity'. They would continually roll over. This would be true of your payables as well. Your suppliers would not want to be paid either. Under this new paradigm, the worth of you or your company would not be the cash in the bank, but would be the sum of your outstanding 'I.O.U. s' less your outstanding payables. This might be ok if you are selling to the U. S. government, but how do you value these outstanding I.O.U. s and payables in the real world over a long period of time?

Enter – the hypothetical '**IOU Bank**'. The I.O.U. BANK would be a nationally recognized institution that kept track of every company and individual's 'Payment Quality Index – PQI' from birth till death. The PQI would be a publically available piece of information established at the same time as the corporation number or personal Social Security Number is established. It would keep track of every transaction of your life or business to determine the quality of the payments you owe, and therefore how likely you are to pay someone else. Since most companies would never want to be paid now, net worth would be the result of the payments owed multiplied by the PQI of the payer, less the payables over the appropriate time period. This would be true for individuals, companies, and countries.

NET WORTH = (Receivables x PQI aggregate of the payers) - PAYABLES

Up until now, this concept would never be possible because of the immense computing power required to perform all these calculations and store them securely for ever. That is one of the reasons why people have tended to use cash or cash substitutes. However in the future of big data, this is simply one more 'killer application' waiting be developed. In the future world of deflation, the I.O.U. Bank is one big idea waiting to happen.

Income Tax is Abolished!!

The problem that a government has in periods of low or negative inflation is that their revenues don't increase as fast as they would like. If incomes are not increasing, income taxes are not increasing and that means that they must find additional ways to generate tax revenues. One way to do that is with asset taxes or wealth taxes. These taxes can take many forms including estate taxes, property taxes, wealth taxes and inheritance taxes. These type of taxes are especially effective because they tend not to affect the large voting middle classes. They are also effective because they generate revenue even if wages go down.

To do this you might pay a fee at the end of the year based upon how much cash you have in the bank. They could possibly do this by maintaining the the tax on income, and applying *new taxes on assets*. They could do this quarterly or monthly. So if you kept your money in the bank, you might lose one or two percent per year to taxes. That would be a tremendous incentive to go buy that new commercial building or rental property. Another concept they could explore is a lottery concept where your social insurance number is pulled out at random and taxes are applied. That way they could only charge tax on one in ten taxpayers but scare everybody into action. Asset and estate taxes could be the next big deflation-fighting battleground.

The reason asset taxes might work is that they can be massive. They can be the weapons of 'Mass Deflation Destruction' the government is looking for. The problem with income taxes and sales taxes is that their basic existence is counter to what we are trying to do. The government is trying to induce spending, but income and sales taxes tend to curtail spending. And as middle agers grow from earners to savers, they don't earn income anyway, but they have assets. Taxing their income may not affect them, but taxing assets could scare them into action. Who said that we have to place our tax burden on incomes anyways?

If asset taxes kick in, I have only been able to think of three ways to reduce your tax bill. One way would be to sell your house and convert all your assets into cash and store them offshore. The second way would be to use this cash to buy physical gold bars and store them in a safety deposit box. (If this idea catches on globally, be prepared to see gold make a run to the top hard and fast.) The third way would be to write yourself a bank draft and don't cash it. Store it in a safety box and bring it out in chunks as you need it. That way you still have easy access to it, but it is out of the hands of prying eyes. Remember, asset taxes can be a debilitating factor on your financial wellbeing. They will start slowly like fees or property taxes. But they can move very quickly to wealth or estate taxes. It is best to be prepared.

Caution: The Inflation Snowball Scenario

As a word of caution, please remember that few of the concepts discussed above have been proven. Although I see many years of global deflation ahead, the governments around the world are desperately trying like to err on the side of too much stimulus and inflation can sometimes be just a matter of confidence. If the building I am looking to buy is going to decline by 3 percent per year you will have a hard time enticing me to buy it at any price. But if I think that negative interest rates or an asset tax is going to shock other investors into action I may decide to move more quickly. A strong dose of confidence may be all that is required to get the animal spirits to come back with a vengeance and create yet another bubble. As much as government authorities are pouring on the fuel, they need to have the extinguisher ready as well. Although it is not my base case scenario, with all this stimulus lying around, it would not take much for inflation to begin snowballing again.

Exit Wounds - The End of Democracy?

The scary part of this whole discussion of inflation, deflation and the associated remedies is the large numbers of unknowns. No one really knows for sure what is about to happen next. Many of the major factors in the various economic models are all experimental. For example the whole European Union is new. It is an experiment designed with the noble objective of unifying a group of historically competitive countries. The fiscal part or the equation has never been put to the test. The massive use of 'Quantitative Easing' is new and the whole concept of zero or negative interest rates is brand new. All of our models developed over the past thirty years are based upon population growth additional leveraging and inflation. In our current world of deleveraging we are not really sure of what we are doing and what comes next. That makes the whole exercise very interesting, and perhaps somewhat frightening.

What makes it even more interesting is the Exit Strategy. Although we are not certain of what is happening now, we are even less sure of how we exit this world of hyper stimulus, or even if we ever do. If the de-leveraging is complete in five to ten years, and our stimulus programs begin to have an effect, how do we exit from the recent decades of huge annual deficit and debt levels? As you can see from our previous discussions, even capping debt levels at fixed amounts will feel like a recession, because, as we discussed, real stimulus only comes when debt levels are growing.

Perhaps the U.S. and European governments will find a way to cut expenses and balance their budgets. Perhaps they will then find a little more funding and a way to pay back their loans. But as we can see from our small town example, if you can't save money when times are good, it can be impossible to put some money aside during times of austerity. Even former Chairman of the Federal Reserve has said recently on CNBC television that we will not be able to exit this strategy without some pain. He did not elaborate.

Escape Velocities

There are three key ways that a country can exit from a situation of extensive debt obligations. The first is that it can go through austerity measures, reduce costs and pay back the loans over time. The second is to default on its debts and obligations. The third is to print money to maximum capacity, devalue its currency against competitive nations and inflate its way out of the problem.

The first solution is the simplest mathematical solution, since the numbers are fairly easy to calculate. However there are questions as to whether this will ever be possible for a democratic country to muster the resolve for the tough measures required. The leadership would be voted out before the austerity measures could be implemented. Nobody would vote in a government that promised hardship for many years to come. The voters may never stand for it. This option may never work in a democratic country. This option may only be viable for an 'un-democratic' country. An example of where severe austerity was implemented and worked was in the 'un-democratic' country, Latvia. Latvia is a Baltic country that rose from the ashes of extreme debt after eight years of austerity. Latvia cut spending so much that it risked denting the social safety net. Latvia then fell into a slump that caused it to lose almost twenty percent of it's economic output. The government's cuts to benefits and public-works were designed to push Latvians back into employment. The finance Minister Andris Vilks said that there was an increasing number of people who didn't want to work. He said some people were coming to work in very nice cars to ask for money. Draconian measures were needed to get back on the right track. But the cuts were so deep that that the International Monetary Fund stated publically that Latvia had gone too far. Latvia developed the worst level of inequality in the European Union causing people to flee the country in 2012 at a rate of 5 percent per year. Nevertheless the Baltic country paid off it's $9.9 billion rescue loan before any other country, and went on with business as usual. Latvia's budget deficit was set to narrow to 1.4 percent of GDP in 2013 from about 9.8 percent in 2009, truly a formidable achievement. But, is there any democratic government in the world that would survive such desperate measures? Possibly not. This may be a solution only viable in un-democratic countries.

The second option is to default on your debts and obligations. In this scenario, the country effectively "gives up". After years of austerity, it realizes that it has built up more debt than it an aver pay back and finally capitualizes. It defaults on its obligations and the creditors are left in distress. The eventual outcome for the country is bleak. The creditors strip the country of everything valuable and then fight over the carcass. This often results in decades of hardship for the unwary citizens. It is the solution of last resort.

A third option for escape from overwhelming debt is to inflate it away. Keep printing more currency to pay for your excesses. That way the value of your currency goes down, your exports go up and you pay off your debts in ever cheaper local currency. That is quite easily done in democracies and doesn't inflame the citizens. Although it does cause inflation and leaves your grandchildren with high debt levels, politicians in developed countries typically choose this option as the path of least resistance.

Democratic solutions

The most likely solution for a democratic country involves a middle ground. It involves some cutbacks and some tax relief and some inflation. Everybody must feel some pain, but not so much that they become enraged. However this comes with it's own risks as well. We can look to Japan for one possible outcome of this middle ground. John Mauldin, the economist, refers to Japan as a bug looking for a windshield. I prefer to think of Japan as a wounded beast very strong and powerful, but becoming more unstable and dangerous. They are still the third largest economy in the world, and if they became unstable that could affect the rest of the world. After accumulating large amounts of debt, they have endured a decade of austerity and deflation. They appear to be a desperate people today willing to take desperate measures. After years of currency appreciation and stability, it is possible that they will attempt to hyper-deflate the yen to increase exports. This may be the only way out for democratic countries. We need to keep an eye on the Japan experiment.

Casino China: The Ultimate Ponzi Scheme

At 1.3 billon, China has the largest population in the world. The overarching goal of the ruling political party is to continue to stay in power. The best way to do this is to keep the population active while continually increasing their wealth. They must maintain full employment and a positive forecast for the future. Doing this for a population that large is a truly daunting task. However, as an autocratic society, their benevolent dictator can implement many programs that a democratic country can't. With this power and responsibility they have so far decided to focus on large infrastructure projects that employ a large number of people. They have focused on large dams, power stations, railroads, buildings and in fact, entire cities. Because of this, they have been consuming commodities such as cement, iron ore, copper and oil at an increasing rates. This has forced commodity prices up all over the world for over a decade. And, because of the big propaganda machine they have created, they can keep local and international messaging alive. Everything is great and growing! However, there are a few cracks in the façade.

One of the big advantages of big infrastructure spending is that it immediately creates it's own market. If you build a big electric generating dam, you need to build a big cement plant.

If you build a big cement plant, you will need lots of steel. So then you need a big steel plant which needs copper. Then you need to build big buildings and cities to house all the workers. And since you will need more electricity to run the plants and the buildings, you almost need to start your second electric generating dam right now! Then you need a stock market so that the employees have somewhere to put their newly earned cash and feel prosperous. And the government keeps the statistics to show how well everything is going. The result is an ever increasing over-supply of things that people actually don't need.

An example of this oversupply has ended up with the many 'Ghost Towns' of China. The Chinese government has created multi-year plans to move rural citizens into the cities. They believed the philosophy of 'build it and they will come'. Well, they have built the big cities, and many people have become wealthy in the building phase, but the people are not coming. They have created big cities with office towers and condominiums that are sitting empty. This Chinese creativeness has even led them to develop 'replica cities' of famous names around the world! Consider the business center of Tianjin, supposedly a replica of Manhattan with a knock-off of the Rockefeller Center and its own Hudson River. It was billed as the world's largest financial center when its ten year construction program was conceived five years ago. Today it is missing only the people. All the tall buildings appeared, but new construction has halted and the builders have left town. And now the fifty billion dollar project is heavily in debt. This is merely one example of the ghost cities that exist in China. For years, both national and local governments have pushed non-stop construction at all costs, without concern for the outcome. Now it is time to fill those cities, but there are no people, just buildings. No one is sure if the cities will ever be used, no one is sure what will happen next. One day if you have some spare time, Google 'Ghost cities of China' and then look them up on Google maps. Just like the

'Great Wall of China', they are so big that it appears that you can see them from space. This ultimate Chinese Ponzi Scheme has been built upon the concept of projects ever increasing in size. What happens when we reach the end?

The Chinese Will Learn Too

Along the way, the Chinese have tried to replicate the banking systems and investment tools they see around the world. In fact, they have allowed for, and even encouraged, a large variety of 'shadow investment' entities to develop. These shadow entities are outside the formal banking systems. The central bank has encouraged them to keep money moving at ever faster rates without much oversight. These entities have increased the lending and the leverage to extreme levels. The goal of the government was to meet the national growth rate targets at all costs.

One of the strategies employed to meet this goal was to use propaganda and news feeds to encourage the average investor to buy stocks at all costs. The implication was that the government would not let the average investor fail. This was the Chinese version of the 'Bernanke Put'. People felt that buying stock was patriotic and that they were supporting the Chinese international image, while at the same time, making a good deal of money as the market ran up. The average Chinese investor of 2015 was about to learn the same lesson that I learned as a kid when I was twelve years old. As the market went up over one hundred percent in 2014, the populous was ecstatic. Many investors even borrowed money to buy more stock. This caused euphoria in the investor base. And this caused an even larger leveraging of the financial base.

But in July of 2015, the Chinese stock market (Shanghai Composite Index) crashed over thirty percent from its highest level in a two month period, leaving many investors in a freefall. Like me at an early age, the novice Chinese investors had learned that the anguish suffered in a small crash was much more excruciating than the excitement of the great build up. Many investors had lost their life savings in a few weeks. It was awful.

The Chinese Stock Market is the Lipstick!

What happened next was even more alarming to me. As soon as the market began to fall the Chinese government immediately issued capital controls. For a number of days, many stock listings were pulled from the exchanges and were not allowed to be traded. Brokers were told they were not allowed to sell certain stocks at all, and the shorting of stocks was not allowed by brokerage houses on the threat of imprisonment. When the anguish of the stock market got to be too excruciating for the population, the Chinese government did the same thing we did as kids. They took away the "minus dice". For a short period of time, they took away the ability to lose money in the market. Although it would not change the outcome of the game (the theoretical winner), they found out that everyone had a lot more fun if all the stocks kept going up. The Chinese investors were learning.

At the time of writing of this book, the eventual outcome of this Chinese advance into stock markets has not been realized, but I am deeply concerned that something has gone terribly wrong. Something is not right in the Chinese economy. I think that the speed and response of the Chinese authorities was way too fast and heavy handed for the degree of anguish experienced. I get the feeling that the Chinese authorities are worried. They are out of levers. The stock market was the last great growth innovation. If it failed, it would be very embarrassing. We could be in for massive problems, massive de-leveraging that will impact the world. I expect the Chinese will use any tool they have to prop it up. I expect the Chinese government will buy stocks themselves. When they do that the

Shanghai Stock Exchange will become meaningless. It will have no relationship to the underlying companies who will be desperate. The Shanghai Stock Exchange will be the 'lipstick on the pig'.

MAD China

During the cold war of the 1960's the Soviet Union and the United States began the process of building nuclear warheads and putting them on intercontinental missiles. At first the whole world became frantic at the thought of each country having the power to destroy each other, and possibly the world, with the flip of one switch. Then a strange realization came into focus. In a strange twist of game theory, each side became to realize that if he pulled the trigger first, the other side would automatically respond and both sides would be automatically destroyed. This scenario was called 'Mutually Assured Destruction' or MAD. I believe the same situation is now evolving in Chinese economics.

In August of 2015, the Chinese economy was 'unexpectedly' slowing down, just as the U. S. economy was picking up. The U.S. central bank was considering raising interest rates for the first time in many years to head off future inflation. However, this had the potential of making things worse for the global economy, especially China. Being desperate, the Chinese sent a message to Janet Yellen, the Chair of the U.S. central bank, telling her not to raise U.S. interest rates. They did this by manipulating their currency, the Renminbi. After two decades of pegging their currency to the U.S. dollar, on August 11, and 12, 2015 they shocked the world by lowering the value of their Yuan by a total of three percent. They later called this a mistake that they would correct, but this act of financial warfare sent shock waves through the global market place. For over almost twenty years the Chinese had frozen their currency in relation to the U.S. dollar, until all of a sudden they changed it.

I believe that the Chinese realized that their economy was slowing. For many years the Chinese guaranteed that they would make sure their currency was exactly pegged to the U.S. dollar. Whenever the U.S. dollar would go up or down, the Chinese Yuan would exactly match it. Part of the problem with this situation was that the Yuan had risen about thirty percent in the past year along with the U.S. dollar. Although this increase did not affect the U.S. that much, it had a huge impact on China. The Chinese were becoming uncompetitive against global competitors and losing market share. They could not withstand any more currency appreciation. They could not afford to let the U.S. raise interest rates. So they sent a message directly to the U.S. Central Bank by abruptly lowering the Yuan without notice. They effectively told the Central Bank of the United States that if they increased interest rates, the Chinese would immediately drop the value of the Yuan starting a global price war and sending economic havoc to the U.S. and around the globe. They would ensure Mutual Assured Destruction (MAD) economically. They felt that this strategy worked with the Soviet Union in the 1960's, so they expected it would work again. They are now trying to dictate U.S. interest rate strategy.

Lift-off for GOLD?

If this Chinese MAD strategy works, they will have effectively exported lower interest rates to the U.S. and brought forward another very interesting situation. At the time of writing of this book, it looks like the United States is finally coming out of a decade of financial doldrums. They will be entering a slow phase of rising inflation. At this point in the business cycle, they should be raising interest rates.

If the U.S. central bank raises rates at their next meeting, then we could be in a long downturn for the value of gold and other assets which do not do well in deflationary times. However, in a unique twist of fate, if the Chinese manage to keep U.S.

interest rates artificially low during the next U.S. expansion phase, we may see inflation rise again. We may be entering a long period of 'negative real interest rates', where the interest rates are lower than the inflation rate. If interest rates are eventually forced to go below zero, this could be a lift-off point for many asset classed, especially gold.

The Chinese Have the Pin!

After many decades of global financial leveraging, engineering and experimentation, the world has become hooked on low interest rates and easy money. We are at a tenuous position. The world is slowing down and the world is already leveraged to the max. We are running out of tricks. Currently, since the U.S. seems to be the only country in the world that is showing signs of growth, the world is watching every nuance. With all the leverage in use right now, many economists liken our global situation to a large voluminous bubble stretched to breaking...

...as you can see from the above, the Chinese have the pin!

Chapter 4: How to Profit Now!

In this book, chapter one attempts to remind us how we currently think of deflation. Chapter two then crafts new ways to look at the inflation - deflation continuum. Chapter three builds new inflation-deflation models to help us craft new deflationary visions of the future. Armed with these new visions and models, Chapter four helps us make better educated decisions and profit now. So let us begin!

To truly profit from deflation you must understand *HUBRIS*

Wikipedia defines hubris as 'excessive pride or self-confidence'. In economics, it also helps to think of 'entitlement'. After years of inflation and good fortune, people tend to get overconfident and deserving. For example, if you live in a commodity country you may feel that you are special and that you deserve your good fortune. 'We are a special people. The Creator put this oil in our ground because we are special.' If you ever see this entitlement attitude, people are overconfident and full of hubris. Hubris is found all over the world in all personalities.

This is important to deflation investors because hubris is a very powerful emotional force that will blind the population to change as it occurs. Most investors will not see the change coming either and will continue to deny it to the end. When a major economic change, like deflation, occurs people will change very slowly. That gives the agile investor time to move before the crowd. So take advantage of hubris in others and face the facts. In times of deflation, hubris can be your friend.

Cash is King!

It probably sounds trivial at this point, but let me repeat the obvious. During deflationary times CASH IS KING ! (In global terms this means U.S. cash.) In its most simple form this means to sell everything and put it into U.S. dollars! Everything you own today will be cheaper tomorrow. Renting should replace owning wherever possible. Stocks, real estate, assets, everything will go down. Sell everything and go to cash. But it is not quite that easy, is it.

In general, during periods of deflation it is better to have most of your assets in cash. But that is not necessarily true for everything. You may need some things now, so you need to buy them now. Or like a house, it may too big of a disruption to sell your house and move, especially if you have already taken a loss. Or, depending on the level of deflation, you may be better off buying the asset, or staying in the asset, because that category may never deflate. Remember our continuum, not all things deflate at the same rate. Even in periods of deflation there will be some things on the bell curve that are still inflating. The trick is to realize what they are and never get out of them.

Another good question to ask is 'what currency are you dealing with?' For the purposes of this discussion we will assume that we are dealing with the US dollar. However, if you are dealing with the Aussie dollar or the Japanese yen, things may react quite differently. For example, although there may be 3% deflation in the US, there may be 5% inflation in Japan because they are devaluing the yen so quickly. This would quickly change the analysis and the recommendation. So although, in general it makes sense to move to cash there are numerous examples where the opposite is true.

Deflationary '20/20 Vision'

As I said earlier in order to make decisions on where to invest or not to invest we should all construct at least one scenario of the future that includes deflation. In the Deflationary Vision of the future the internet, 'Big Data' and mobile devices will be prominent. Competition will be global and fierce. Pockets of cooperation will exist regionally for products that don't fit with global competitive model. On average prices will be dropping three percent per year with some items still inflating two to three percent and some deflating ten percent. Wages will be dropping two percent per year, so we are still gaining against deflation. Wages for jobs that can be 'off-shored' will be dropping five percent per year. The forces of deflation could last for decades as the internet continues to deflate and we gradually pay off our bills. After that it is anyone's guess. If the global population continues to increase we may see inflation come back with a vengeance. If not, we may live with deflation for a long, long time.

With this vision as a backdrop, it may now be helpful to let our minds wander and create even more models and visions.

What Comes First - Unemployment or Deflation?

Many people think that high unemployment comes with deflationary times. They are wrong. High unemployment comes just before deflation. This may seem like a trivial distinction, but it will be one of the key indicators to predict when things turn from inflation to deflation and vice versa. Why does it happen this way? To answer this look back and use our San Francisco real estate model. In that model people always want better things. The only thing that holds them back is money. (Remember, you may not agree with this value statement, but this is just a model.) If people had enough money they would continually bid the prices up for all products and services. The reverse is true as well. If they have less money they will not bid up prices and will allocate their limited funds to only the most important priorities. The result is that prices will go down.

Now you may say that this model is just a different version of the old 'supply and demand' model taught in 'economics 101', and it is. The first difference is that this new model carries the attribute of prediction. By modifying the new model I may be able to predict what the inflation rate will be in the future. From my observations it appears to me that when the US unemployment rate goes above 7% we enter a period of deflation. When the unemployment rate is around 6 % inflation is around 1%. When the unemployment rate goes below 5% we may begin to see higher inflation rates around 2 to 4%. The theory behind this is that when there are more jobs, people have more money to spend and they bid prices up, and you get inflation. The actual unemployment rates can be used as a leading indicator of inflation and deflation trends to come. I know I am not the first person to think of this as I assume this is one of the discussions at the quarterly meeting of the Fed. I also think that this is why when the Fed sets an unemployment rate of 6.5%, it is at the same time setting an inflation target of 2% - 3%. So one way to predict future inflation or deflation rates is to track the unemployment rate.

The second difference is that the new models must include wages. If 100 people making $50,000 per year in a high paying oil field job get laid off and then find work at $25,000 per year in a retail outlet, the unemployment rate stays the same but the wages go way down. People will not be bidding up prices if their wages are cut in half. It is total wages that drives the economy. Rather than tracking employment exclusively, economists should also focus on wages.

What If "Net Present Value" Goes In Reverse!

One of the key factors in making a purchase decision is to evaluate how much value you will receive in the future from a purchase you make right now. If the purchase is for immediate consumption the decision can be quite easy. For example, if I am thirsty and I want to buy a bottle of water, I can quickly make a value decision now. But if I want to buy a car to deliver pizza for the next five years, the decision can be more difficult. In the case where the value comes in the future, economists typically discount the future value to take into account inflation. In other words, as a result of future inflation, the $1000.00 that I make in year five is not worth as much as the $1000.00 that I make in year one. To calculate the net value to me right now, (Net Present Value) I add up the future income I will make (discounted for inflation) and subtract the cost of the purchase. If the value is positive, I buy it. If it is negative, I don't.

The same calculation is true for a company trying to decide if they should purchase a piece of equipment. They calculate the Net Present Value. That means that if they buy a piece of machinery to save money, do the annual savings (after accounting for inflation) pay for initial cost. If they spend $1000 dollars for a machine and it creates $100 per year of cost reductions, was that a good decision? They add up the future cost savings (or income) after discounting them for inflation and subtracts the purchase price. That gives a "net present value". If the "net present value" of the purchase adds up to be greater than the cost of the purchase, then the net value is said to be greater than zero and you should buy the machine. This calculation has been ingrained in our business schools and text books for decades. It is the basic law of almost all corporate decisions.

But what happens if you are in a deflation scenario. Future dollars are worth more than present dollars! All the calculations go in reverse....just like our river! If you delay

91

paying for the machine, it will cost you more in terms of current dollars. So pay immediately. By the same token, the money you receive back in year ten is worth more than the money you receive in year one. Ironically, the longer you wait to collect your income, the more it is worth, and the purchase will effectively cost you less. This is actually hard to fathom!

Our financial systems, our calculations, and our laws were never designed with deflation in mind. What would you say to a friend that borrowed money from you and paid you back late? Would you be upset because he was late, or happy that the money he paid back was worth more? Alternatively retailers might advertise "Don't pay for five years!" But don't fall for it. Pay them immediately with your current cheap money. In fact people may want money paid back to them at such a later date, We may enter into a system of credits whereby money never changes hands, just credits. You might say *"You owe me $1000.00 but just keep it for now. Pay me back when you can, the later the better, but I have it on file that you owe it to me"*.

As discussed previously, this may cause us to enter into a form of 'shadow banking system' where people never pay each other but keep tabs on who owes whom. If this is the case, the whole banking and legal systems will have to be re-tooled to handle the new logic. All of our banking calculations will have to be re-evaluated.

The Future of the Retail Mall is 'Showrooms and Phones'

Get over it. The internet has changed everything. Whereas you used to go to a store and look at products and buy things, now you go to the store to look at things and then go home and buy them over the internet. Many retail outlets have become money losing showrooms. Enjoy them while you can, because many of them will not survive. And neither will the malls that house them. Going to the mall for a Saturday afternoon, may be a thing of the past. Instead, we will walk through a few "high end" showrooms for a couple of hours and then go home to shop on line. The hardest hit will be the mid level department stores. Their prices will not match the internet retailers and their cost will be higher. One group of stores that will survive will be the luxury retailers where fit and feel are more important than price. Another group will be the discount and convenience stores where you will walk through and physically pick things up, things you need now.

Retail malls will morph into two groups, high end exclusive malls, and discount malls. With their discount (deflationary?) prices, online retailers like Amazon will own the middle market.

Real Estate: 'Gateway cities and Micro-Pockets'

Real Estate will prove to be the biggest paradox of the deflationary world. That is because it will be reacting to two very large opposing forces. On the one hand real estate will tend to drop in value across the country as the economy slows and jobs are lost. On the other hand, it will tend to rise as the central banks around the world lower interest rates to keep the economy moving. The result will be real estate spikes in cities (and recreational properties) associated with high employment. We will see a real estate decline in traditional manufacturing and remote locations . The expanding cities will tend to be 'Global Gateway' cities where the wealthy and elite of the world will want to travel freely. These cities will tend to have access to education, financial and government facilities. They will be seen as intellectual and high tech cities like London, New York, Paris, Beijing, Berlin and San Francisco . Small towns and cities will not do as well. People from small towns will move to big cities looking for work. They will also be looking to rent their housing. An opportunity for rental properties will emerge in larger cities.

Because these Global Gateway cities will grow, crime and congestion (especially traffic congestion) will become some of the biggest problems for the wealthy inhabitants. Therefore, within these cities, high value 'Micro Pockets' will develop. These micro pockets will be safe areas close to highways, public transportation, education, entertainment and medical facilities. Small micro pockets of the elite will form within Global Gateway cities. Travel time will be the bane of the wealthy, and quality time, the grail.

However, the greatest paradox in the real estate world will emerge when the economy slows down so much that central banks force interest rates into negative territory. On the one hand people will be racing to get their money into real estate and away from bank fees and taxes. Real estate will skyrocket. On the other hand, the government would only do that if the economy was in very bad shape, and job losses were mounting. In this scenario housing prices would skyrocket up until everyone loses their jobs. Then they would drop like a rock. This is the most difficult scenario to plan as it will be almost impossible to time correctly. No one is going to phone you to tell you that the real estate crash is beginning tomorrow. It will just happen. For a quick look at how this may transpire, you just have to look at house prices in oil towns. Prices skyrocketed as the price of oil went up, only to fall again as the layoffs mounted. It can happen in a heartbeat. So, like gold, real estate is bi-polar. Some areas will go up while other areas will go down.

So put on your '**In-deflation** sunglasses' and stay alert.

Hometown Refugees

Over the past century, two of the great drivers of our economy were agriculture and manufacturing. These great economic forces drove people out across the land. The farmers went to where the fields were and the manufacturers went in search the raw materials or cheap power. Quite often they created new urban or rural centers as they spread across the country. In the new scenario with global communications and cheap oil prices it will be more efficient to form manufacturing and farming hubs around the world. People in the local rural centers will begin to lose their jobs. When they begin to look for new employment opportunities they will look in the larger urban centers. They will go to the big cities in search of jobs and a better social safety net. They will be refugees from small hometowns, and they will come in droves. They will not be able to afford homes, so they will be looking for rental facilities. These rental facilities could be either stand alone apartments or rental units of condominium buildings. In the coming deflationary world, people may not be able to afford homes and rental properties may be in high demand, therefore increasing rental prices. If rental rates go up it may mean that people are moving from small towns to big cities in search of work. Paradoxically, higher rental rates may not be an indication of inflation, but could be an early indicator of deflation.

Why is Gold Bipolar?

Gold is the least understood of all the commodities. People have made and lost fortunes trying to predict the future price of gold. The pundits all provide conflicting reasons as to why the price of gold does or does not increase. I have never found them very useful. I have developed my own models to deal with the situation. Only time will tell if I am right or wrong. In essence I believe that gold is very difficult to understand because it is bi-polar. By that I mean that it can behave differently depending on the circumstances. Just like water above freezing is soft and liquid and below freezing it is hard and brittle, gold can behave in two different ways as well and have completely different properties. It can behave either like a hedge against inflation, or a currency of last resort.

First I will discuss it as a hedge against inflation. I first began to explore this theory when I heard the story of an old woman that ran a bakery during the great deflationary depression. A loaf of bread cost 5 cents. (So cash was king!) A man came up to her and said he had no money. He begged for a loaf of bread for his family. She said no, and that it wasn't fair to the other patrons who had to pay money. He then took off his gold Rolex watch and offered that as payment. She again said no politely. She then reached into a drawer below and pulled out a box full of dusty gold Rolex watches. She said she didn't need any more gold Rolex watches. She needed cash. Gold was of limited value to her. I am not sure how true this story is, but it left an indelible image on my mind and started me down the path of calculating the correct price of gold.

Starting with the assumption that gold would lose its value in deflationary times I looked for data to support the fact that gold goes up with inflation. I was told a story about an ounce of gold buying a suit of armor in Roman times and that it still buys a decent suit today. That made sense to me and I stared to believe that if inflation went up, gold would go right along with it. I then noticed that gold bounced up and down as governments adjusted interest rates. So I looked for correlations there. What I found was quite interesting. I found data to suggest that the price of gold was highly correlated with 'negative real interest rates'. That would mean that the price of gold would go up whenever 'real interest rates' were negative. That means that if interest rates were 4% but inflation was 5% percent, that would mean that real interest rates were negative and then gold would go up. If inflation stayed the same but interest rates went to 6%, then gold would go down. The price of gold seemed to go up if interest rates were lower that the inflation rate. For all intents and purposes, gold had no intrinsic usage or value. So if it costs you money to hold it, there is no reason to own it. If everybody comes to believe this same rational over time, then it becomes a self-fulfilling prophecy. In this case it acts like an apartment

96

building. If you expect the apartment building to be worth 5% more tomorrow, and interest rates were 4%, then your 'effective interest rate' would be negative and you would buy the building. If interest rates went up or the future value of the building was only 3% more, then you wouldn't buy it.

I have often heard that gold is a 'store of value'. I believe that is the case today. In one of its forms, gold is a way to protect people from inflation, or expected inflation, depending on real interest rates. I say expected inflation because the price of gold went up substantially from $1200 per ounce to $1900 per ounce when QE 1, 2 and 3 were announced in the United States and interest rates went to zero. In this case people expected QE to generate inflation or even hyper-inflation with no interest rate to speak of. Negative real interest rates would shoot sky high, and gold prices would follow. But as people began to realize that there are many other factors required besides QE to generate inflation and that inflation might never come, the gold prices began to drop. One of the reasons this correlation is so hard to notice is that the price of gold went up on the assumption of future inflation, not inflation itself. So if a historian looks back on the data in future years, and sees the price came down even as interest rates were low, he would see a distortion in the trend. Therefore I believe one of the interpretations of gold is as a store of value protected against inflation.

Some of the ideas expressed above can be found in the literature that discusses gold prices. I would like to add "currency fluctuation" as one important and overlooked nuances to the prediction of gold prices. Most of the global population lives outside of the U.S. and transacts in their local currency. However the price of gold is measured in U.S. dollars. To a prospective gold purchaser in a country that has devalued their currency, the price of gold appears to go up. If gold goes up in terms of local currency, they are able to buy less and there is less demand. However, in a country that has increased the value of their currency, gold appears to be cheaper and they can buy more, thus increasing demand. Many of the countries with high currency fluctuations are commodity countries.

So the final nuance I would like to add to global gold price prediction is to add a factor that takes into account the value of commodities. Gold will go up if there are negative real interest rates in the United States, and will go higher faster if commodity inflation erupts at the same time.

The "Expected Value" of Gold

The second way that gold behaves is as a 'currency of last resort'. Some people mistake this with 'safe haven' status, but I have not found this to be the case. When people are looking for a safe haven, they tend to move toward the U.S. dollar or the Swiss Franc. They only move toward gold when they think the US dollar is at risk. In that case I interpret gold as the 'currency of last resort' situation. With this scenario there comes a strange paradox.

Imagine that I had a coin that was legal tender under certain conditions with the bank. The coin had one side that was emblazoned with a bald eagle. The other side was smooth. The bank said that they would redeem to the holder one dollar on the condition that the coin was flipped in front of the teller. If the bald eagle turned up you would get a dollar. If the smooth side turned up you would forfeit the coin. Now how much is the coin worth to an outside investor? If you had a thousand coins how much would an outside investor pay you for each coin? The correct answer is 50 cents, even though the coin will never actually be worth that amount. It will be only worth a dollar or nothing, never 50 cents. An investor will pay fifty cents because that is its expected value. Over 1000 coins he would expect to flip $500. Now if that coin started to wear out over time so that it landed showing the eagle only forty percent of the time, an investor might pay you forty cents each. That coin is only worth its expected value.

Gold sometimes acts like this as well. In its raw state gold has very few uses except for jewelry. However, if all fiat currencies (mostly the U.S. dollar) were to collapse, gold could replace paper and be legal tender. In this case gold would be 'the currency of last resort'. For the purpose of this model let's assume that its value as jewelry tends toward zero. However its value as currency can be quite high. Jim Rikards in his book Currency Wars shows one option where if all the currency in the world was converted to gold, the price of gold could be worth $6000 per ounce. If all the currency in the world stayed as is and gold was never required then gold would tend toward zero. So it is possible to think of gold in a bi-modal way just like our coin. If calamity hits our economic system gold would be worth $6,000 per ounce. If the U.S. dollar survives, gold will be worthless. So using this model, gold is just a reflection of how well the world thinks the US dollar is going to do. If the US collapses then gold is worth $6000. If the US survives, then gold is worth zero. So if gold is at $2000, what does that tell us about the probabilities that investors are putting on a collapse? The implied answer is 30%.

I use a combination of these two models to calculate an appropriate value for gold. Over the few years, the U.S. economy has been improving, their Quantitative Easing program has been terminated and they are threatening to raise interest rates. However, as you will see in the scenario planning section, I think we may be entering into a phase of negative real interest rates. In this case gold could shoot up to $6000 in a hurry. I wish I could offer a more definitive outlook for gold, but at least armed with these models you will be able to make quick decisions in the future.

How Much Would You Pay For an Extra Year of Life?

…'The value of time inflates over time!,

We have focused on the many different aspects of inflation and deflation and how to make money, but what about one of the most important assets we all have, our lifespan. It helps us to wrap up our discussion by adding a little perspective here. Consider the following situation.

If someone said that you could start your next vacation in one year plus a week, would you pay more to have the time shortened by one week? Probably not. But what if someone said that you could start your vacation today instead of next week, would you pay for that? Probably. Why? (It is still only a week.)

People place distorted values on time. Our time right now seems to be more valuable than our time in the future. As time gets closer to now, it gets more expensive. It inflates. In addition, as we get older time inflates. When you were young with many days ahead of you time seems like something far away. However, when you get older, each day takes on significantly more meaning. As you age, you would probably pay more for an extra day of life. While everything is deflating, time will always inflate.

As you begin to deal with everything deflation, make sure you remember one of the most important concepts: 'The value of time inflates over time.' Be sure you take time for your body and your soul.

How to Profit Now with your... wait for it... 'Personal prescription *In-deflation Sunglasses*'

So now we have come to the ultimate question of this book. How do we profit from all of this? As you suspected, it helps to put on your sunglasses. But they are not just sunglasses any more. Through the course of this book we have learned that deflation is really just part of an in-deflation continuum. We have also learned that all products and services will 'in-deflate' at their own rate. Finally we have learned that each of us will have our own unique in-deflation rate because of our age, or where we live. In effect each of us will have our own "prescription" sunglasses.

In effect each of us has our own 'Personal Prescription In-Deflation Sunglasses' (PPIS). This is the more efficient model that I use to look at the future. Wear your PPIS when you look at economics around the globe. See if they help you as much as they help me.

Specifically, here are the top ideas to maximize your wealth in times of deflation. Please read them through the lenses of your personal sunglasses. Everybody's situation is different.

Service Inflation and Commodity Deflation

......A Once-In-a-Lifetime Opportunity!

The world is in the middle of a massive de-leveraging and deflationary period. However, each country is in a different phase of the process. The United States began the process during the great recession of 2008. There were a massive number of jobs lost and housing prices tumbled. This U.S.

slowdown greatly affected the rest of the world which in turn began to slow down as well. Europe addressed the problem by deflating their currency and the Chinese addressed the problem with a massive infrastructure buildup. The massive infrastructure build-up in China required unprecedented amounts of commodities such as oil, steel, and copper. This caused commodity prices and commodity currencies to rise abnormally. Commodity producers replied with huge increases in capacity. By 2014 this heightened pace of economic activity was what we came to believe as normal.

Over many decades, the U.S. has evolved into mostly a service based economy, with smokestack and manufacturing industries moving offshore. In 2015, after seven years of slow recovery, the U.S. economy began to show signs of life. At the same time, the great Chinese commodity boom was beginning to slow down. If you assume that it takes a decade for the full impact of de-leveraging to work its way through a country's economic system, then the U.S. is now beginning to pull out of its malaise while China will be in it for another ten years. What we are now seeing a diverging trend in our "In-deflation" situation. The U.S. service sector should begin to experience increasing modest inflation, while the smokestack and commodity sectors should continue to experience significant deflation. The usual outcome of this situation would be modest overall inflation of one to two percent per year. Then, as inflation increased, the U.S. central bank would normally increase interest rates in an effort to keep everything in balance. However, MAD China changed everything.

As discussed in chapter three, on August 11,2015 the Chinese let their currency devalue briefly sending a message to the U.S. central bank saying that if they increased U.S. interest rates, China would devalue the Yuan and causing global commodity deflation and wreak havoc in world financial markets. On August 26, 2015 the fed responded when the New York Fed president William Dudley said that arguments for a September rate hike were less compelling than they were only a few weeks ago. The Chinese message was received. The U.S. central bank had now accepted the mandate to be the central bank to the world. As such, they would keep interest rates lower than they normally would be if they were just focusing on the U.S. economy. I believe that this small event, unnoticed by most people in the world, changed everything. I believe this has created a "once-in-a-lifetime" opportunity for long-term negative real interest rates in the United States. Just like our kid's game, the U.S. central bank had just taken away the '**Minus Dice**' for the world!

For the everyday investor this means that commodities should continue their slow deflationary downturn as we work through the global oversupply of capacity, however the service sectors should get a boost. We are now entering a period of 'service inflation and commodity deflation'. (Some people may refer to this as 'Smokestack deflation'.) Since the largest services sector in the world is in the United States, this should usher in a decade of accelerated growth in services sector in the United States as never seen before. The U.S. could become one of the few 'Inflation Islands' in the world, offering a 'once in a lifetime opportunity'. But life is never that simple is it.

Scenario Planning

Although all the pundits will tell you otherwise, the world is too complicated to predict with complete accuracy. In situations like this it is helpful to use the scenario planning tools discussed earlier. In a traditional scenario planning session the planners start with a base case scenario which is the scenario that is considered to be most likely. Then a worst case scenario is developed, where it is assumed that everything goes bad, and then a best case scenario where everything is great. Finally a few alternative scenarios are added to keep the planners aware of other developments.

In my opinion, the <u>main objective of scenario planning is survival</u>. Although your overall plan is to come up with the most profitable strategy, ultimately you must never implement a plan that could wipe you out. You must, above all else, live to fight another day! With these caveats in mind, I start with the base case scenario and then look to the worst case scenario. Only after I spend considerable time on these two scenarios do I turn my attention to the best case scenario. Finally, I craft alternative scenarios that will help me keep 'my eyes open' to unexpected developments. If the unexpected developments are significant, I start the process over. The reader is free to develop as many scenarios as possible. In this discussion I will only describe two scenarios. I will briefly describe the 'worst case' scenario, but I will only develop an action plan for the 'base case' scenario.

Base Case Scenario: ' Negative Interest Rates – Save the Day! '

The base case should be the most likely scenario. To simplify this scenario I will separate the world into three major trading blocks, the U.S., Europe, and China. In my base case, I will start by assuming the world economies are not connected. If that were true, the U.S. would slowly emerge from its recession and enter a decade long growth phase of prosperity supported by low interest rates (forced upon them by the Chinese). This would offer investors the 'once in a lifetime' opportunity previously discussed. I also believe that Europe would struggle in and out of deflation for a considerable time and that China would enter their decade of deflation which would severely affect commodities.

However, the global economy <u>is connected</u>. What happens on one side of the planet affects the other. Therefore, when I build global factors into the scenario and I modify my base case, the decade of U.S. prosperity still occurs, but is delayed about five years. Under this global set of assumptions, China shrinks, causing commodities to implode and drags Europe into a multi-year deflationary period. Although the U.S. is mostly a service economy, it is still affected. Instead of pulling out of their malaise in 2016, the U.S. is dragged back down for another five years or so. After the five year period, the world adjusts to all the changes and the U.S. is propelled forward to another decade of prosperity. Since this will be five years away, I call this the next great American decade 'to come'. It will happen, and it will be great. It will just be delayed a bit. All we have to do first is deal with our five year deflationary spiral problem. Unfortunately, that will be a very big problem indeed.

To deal with the global deflationary problem, the U.S. Federal reserve will not only have to reverse its intentions and scale back any plans to increase interest rates, but it will have to take drastic action. Since Europe has proven that more Quantitative easing has limited results, the Fed will have to begin to experiment with negative interest rates. This will be a problem because it is so new to everyone. The world will scramble to deal with all the 'new plumbing'. This will mean that the economy is slowing and unemployment will rise. Stocks and commodities will begin to drop. The U.S. dollar will begin to drop but gold will skyrocket. Real estate will initially go up until unemployment increases and then go down except in global gateway cities.

Although the global deflationary period would normally last ten years, the U.S., and its service economy will be the first country to pull out after only five years. Then they will enter their decade of prosperity. Since the base case discussed has such a dramatic change in direction, you will see that I have separated the action plans into Phase 1 and Phase 2, each with its own strategy and action plans.

Worst Case Scenario

In the worst case scenario I see China drawing the whole world into a deflationary spiral for a number of years. Commodity prices drop, jobs are lost, and global trade slows, while governments struggle to pay off their debts. Global unrest increases. Refugees move to find employment and social safety nets. Stock markets and governments tumble. All the countries try to devalue their currencies and create local inflation and U.S. cash is king! The U.S. does not emerge from the malaise, and the global deflationary spiral lasts for decades.

Although I don't see this as the most likely scenario, it is useful to consider since it encourages us to use a little caution as we move forward, and it also addresses many of the same issues we address in Phase 1 of our Base Case. Remember, the primary objective of scenario planning is survival. So based upon this discussion here are my recommended action plans for Phase 1 and Phase 2 of our Base Case.

Action Plans!

BASE CASE: 'Negative Interest Rates – Save the Day!

Phase 1 (Years 0- 5): 'Global Deflationary Period'

U.S. succumbs to global deflation, corporate profits tumble, and unemployment rises. The Fed tries more Q. E. with limited success and then resorts to negative interest rates. Under this scenario only commodity currencies will fall faster that the U.S. dollar will fall. Under this scenario, Cash is King ! Gold will be the King of Cash !

1. Sell your stocks as commodity deflation will drag down all stocks.

2. Exchange commodity currencies for U.S. Dollars.

3. Always make decisions in U.S. Dollars (the only 'global currency')

4. Sell or downsize your home (except possibly in Global Gateways).

5. Buy thirty year U.S. T-bills as interest rates will slowly drop.

6. Buy gold. It will rise with the next U.S. Q.E. program.

    (It will skyrocket if real interest rates go negative!)

7. Rent, don't buy assets that depreciate.

8. Shelter your assets before asset taxes are imposed.

i. Write yourself a bank draft and put it in a safety deposit box.

ii. Buy physical gold and put it in your safety deposit box.

9. Pay now, never later (your money will be worth more later).

10. Lend, don't borrow (for the reason noted above).

11. Large corporations should investigate the 'IOU Bank' concept.

12. Watch for the turnaround to Phase 2!

Phase Two (Years 5 – 15): 'The great American Decade to Come'

After five years you will see that the commodity chaos has worked through the system and the U.S. will become one of the few global 'islands of inflation'. Assets will escalate in price, and because of MAD China, the U.S. Central Bank will keep interest rates lower than they would otherwise be for many years to come. Since you will be flush with cash from the decisions you made in Phase 1, this will era of asset expansion will provide you the opportunity of a lifetime!

1. Don't fight the Fed. Borrow money to buy appreciating assets

2. Buy U.S. stocks that serve mainly the United States services sector. Eg.

   – Buy U.S. stocks that benefit from recreation or lower commodities

   – hHotels, airlines or oil refiners

3. Invest in U.S. retirement and healthcare opportunities.

4. Buy into the upcoming residential real estate boom! Buy U.S. real estate in **Gateway Cities** and recreational areas, preferably in **Micro-pockets.**

5. Buy rental properties in or near gateway cities, or educational facilities.

6. Sell your T-bills as interest rates will slowly go up

7. Sell your gold and use it to purchase the assets discussed above.

8. Manage "time-life" inflation: Take care of your body and your mind

9. Put on your Tin Foil Hat and Embrace "Global In-Deflation". It is not evil, it is just different.

10. Drop the hubris, put on your own "Personal Prescription In-deflation Sunglasses" and make your own decisions.

11. Opportunity abounds!

Summary

In this book I have introduced a number of new economic topics that I think are very important but that are not in the mainstream of economic thought. I think they are important because they can change the way we all look at global inflation and deflation and cause us to make financial decisions completely different from before. Many ideas in this book have never been fully explored because they are contrary to the standard global economic models espoused by mainstream economists. They go against the classical thinking required to keep countries and politicians in stable positions. I have tried to introduce these topics in the form of simple visual models like rivers and bell curves in order to bring them to life. I have introduced the concept of a "Global In-deflation continuum" and tried to show how each country and each individual, is separate and yet interconnected. Then I have created the concept of an advanced form of 'Deflation Sunglasses' to help us look through the morass of economic detail and make sense of the real messages. Armed with these new models, I have tried to give the reader the unique visionary powers to forecast inflation, deflation and global economics well into the future. With these new powers, I hope the reader will be better able to make his or her own personal decisions.

I believe that the last four or five decades of global leveraging has given rise to an unsustainable global economic level that we now refer to as 'the norm'. I believe that we are entering a period of new norms. If the United Sates were an economy isolated from the world, I believe that it would continue to prosper, albeit at a slow growth rate. I believe that the Eurozone experiment would survive and muddle along, but on a smaller scale. And I believe the Chinese would drift into a long period of deflation which would cause domestic unrest beyond a level that they could tolerate.

However, we are not isolated economies any more. We are all part of one big global economy. Each country is moving along its own 'In-deflation Bell Curve' at a different rate, but we are all connected. What happens on one side of the world definitely impacts the other side of the world. The big risk to the global economy is the Chinese economic bubble which extends into their real estate, manufacturing, commodity and banking sectors. It is now showing signs of crumbling, and could push the already weak global economy into a multi-decade deflationary period. Responding to Chinese pressure, the U.S. Central Bank now considers China 'Too Big to Fail'. In order to avoid a devaluation of the Yuan and global economic chaos, the U.S. central bank has tacitly agreed to become the 'Central Bank of the World. They have indicated that they will keep interest rates abnormally low for an extended period of time. Although this will not stop the deflationary period in its tracks, it will allow the U.S. and its service economy to recover faster, and usher in the next economic boom.

I am not an economist or a financial planner. I am just an observer with a passion for modelling. The ideas expressed in this book are just my personal thoughts from my personal experiences. I bring them forward as provocative discussion points for the reader in order to help promote debate. In the last chapter of this book I have suggested some specific actions to take right now in order to maximize profits. They are just suggestions. Please contact your financial planner before you make your own decisions.

Because the ideas in this book are so un-traditional, I don't expect everyone will adopt all of them, or any of them, immediately. What I have tried to do is to introduce a new way to think, a new way to look at the world, and a whole new realm of possibilities. It is my hope that, with this new perspective, and these new tools, the reader will be well prepared to make his own decisions as time marches on.

Once you see the models and recommendations slowly come to real life in the marketplace, you will begin to gain confidence in fully implementing them and fully dealing with the topic of global in-deflation.

However, a word of warning. Before you try to fully grasp the change that will be happening all around you, I would ask that you consider that you may already be full of the debilitating "hubris bug". Most of the people I talk to about deflation get angry with me. They feel like I am personally taking shots at them for their many years of poor financial decisions, from stocks to real estate. This is not the case. I am not trying to condemn   people, decisions, or situations. I am merely trying to show the reader that other economic models should be considered within the portfolio of options. To understand the implications of deflation, you will eventually realize that you need to step away from the situation before you will be able to grasp it.

To **fully** profit from deflation, you must fully understand hubris. You must express extreme humility and understand that you don't **deserve** anything. Nothing is owed to you because you are special. The economy is just a numbers game. It moves and flows mathematically. You are just a piece of it. You must relinquish yourself to the mathematics. And also remember that, like when we were kids, we found out that losing was ten times more stressful than winning. When you fully understand this, you will begin to know how to deal with global deflation. You will know that that global debt reduction and de-leveraging is way more difficult and stressful that global leveraging. It is similar to what they say about 'Hotel California'. Once you get into debt, it is very painful to get out.

For the fleet of foot, this next fifteen years will offer 'islands' of great opportunity. We will move from five years of debilitating deflation into the inflationary years of 'The next Great American Decade to Come.' Armed with your 'Personal

Prescription In-deflation Sunglasses' (PPIS) you will be able to lead the way to prosperity.

So go ahead. Try them on!

About the Author

Mike Verge was born in Montreal, Quebec, Canada to an American mother and a Canadian father. He graduated from electrical engineering from the University of Toronto and got his MBA from Wilfrid Laurier University in Waterloo, Ontario. As a dual citizen, he has held a number of executive positions in both Canadian and American corporations. During his time in the oil and gas pipeline industry, he travelled the globe extensively growing businesses. With his electrical engineering and MBA experience, and as a past member of Mensa, he is uniquely qualified to identify trends, visualize patterns and bring them all to life.

He is married, has two adult children, and lives in Toronto, Canada. His hobbies include sports, economics, history and geology.

References:

Buffett, W. (2003). *Warren Buffett's Letters To Berkshire Shareholders 1977-2002*. Retrieved from http://www.berkshirehathaway.com/letters/2002.html .

Coates, J. (2012). *The Hour Between Dog and Wolf: How Risk-Taking Transforms Us, Body and Mind*. Random House Canada.

Dent, H. (2012). A Decade of Volatility: Demographics, Debt and Deflation. *The Market Oracle*. Retrieved from http://www.marketoracle.co.uk/Article36464.html.

Dorn, J. (2012, December 27). Ben Bernanke's QE4: Another Step Towards Helicopter Money, And Away From Freedom. *Forbes*. Retrieved from http://www.forbes.com/sites/jamesdorn/2012/12/27/ben-bernankes-qe4-another-step-toward-helicopter-money-and-away-from-freedom/

Ferguson, N. (2011). *Civilization: The West and the Rest*. London, UK: Penguin.

Gates, B., Myhrvold, N., & Rinearson, P. (1995). *The road ahead. New York and London: Penguin Books*.

Glasser, S. P. (2008). *Essentials of clinical research*. New York: Springer.

Huxley, J. (1927). The Tissue-Culture King. *Amazing Stories*, (Vol. 2, no. 5, pp. 451–59).

Jahan, S., Mahmud, A.S., & Papageorgiou, C. (2014). What is Keynesian Economics? *Finance & Development*. Retrieved from http://www.imf.org/external/pubs/ft/fandd/2014/09/basics.htm

Mauldin, J., & Tepper, J. (2011). *Endgame: the end of the debt supercycle and how it changes everything*. Hoboken, NJ: John Wiley & Sons.

Niewiroski, R. (2007). *RayBanAviator* [Image File]. Retrieved from http://www.projectrich.com/gallery, via https://commons.wikimedia.org/wiki/File:RayBanAviator.jpg#/media/File:RayBanAviator.jpg

Patterson, S. (2012). Dark pools: The rise of the machine traders and the rigging of the US stock market. New York, NY: Crown Business.

Porter, M. E. (2008). *Competitive strategy: Techniques for analyzing industries and competitors*. New York: Free Press.

Ramer, H. (2011). *The Provincial Letters: Blaise Pascal (1623–1662)*. ERIS Etext Project. Retrieved from http://infomotions/etexts/id/pascal-provinvial-570

Rickards, J. (2011). *Currency wars: The making of the next global crisis*. New York, NY: Penguin.

www.ingramcontent.com/pod-product-compliance
Lightning Source LLC
Chambersburg PA
CBHW022111210326
41521CB00028B/308